MASTERING THE ART OF
Solution-Focused
Counseling

JEFFREY T. GUTERMAN

AMERICAN COUNSELING ASSOCIATION
5999 Stevenson Avenue
Alexandria, VA 22304
www.counseling.org

MASTERING THE ART OF
Solution-Focused
Counseling

10 9 8 7 6 5 4 3 2

American Counseling Association
5999 Stevenson Avenue
Alexandria, VA 22304

Director of Publications
Carolyn C. Baker

Production Manager
Bonny E. Gaston

Cover design by Scot Howard

Author photograph by Fabiola Garcia

Library of Congress Cataloging-in-Publication Data
Guterman, Jeffrey T.
  Mastering the art of solution-focused counseling/Jeffrey T. Guterman.
    p. cm.
  Includes bibliographical references.
  ISBN 1-55620-267-9 (alk. paper)
  ISBN 978-1-55620-267-4 (alk. paper)
  1. Solution-focused therapy.   I. Title.
RC489.S65G88   2006
616.89´14—dc22   2005034210

To my *Nana,* Ida Wolk

TABLE OF CONTENTS

Foreword vii
Preface ix
Acknowledgments xix
About the Author xxi

Chapter 1 ■ Introduction 1

Chapter 2 ■ A Postmodern Perspective 9

Chapter 3 ■ Problems and Change 21

Chapter 4 ■ Before the First Session 35

Chapter 5 ■ The First Session 45

Chapter 6 ■ After the First Session 57

Chapter 7 ■ Treating Depression 69

Chapter 8 ■ Substance Problems 83

Chapter 9 ■ Grief, Suicide, Trichotillomania, and Other Problems 95

Chapter 10 ■ Jared's Complaint 111

Chapter 11 ■ The Future of Solution-Focused Counseling 123

References 131
Index 145

FOREWORD

I n 1995, I received an unexpected telephone call from a counselor
by the name of Jeffrey T. Guterman. He called to say that he had
resonated to my Developmental Counseling and Therapy (DCT)
approach. But right away Guterman began to challenge me. He
suggested that my constructivist–developmental perspective did not
seem to adequately account for the social constructionist position that
he considered integral to our field. Needless to say, I disagreed with
him and pointed out the interactive and multicultural dimensions of
DCT. This was to be the first of many stimulating conversations that
Guterman and I would have about critical issues in counseling.

I did not know it then, but at the time Guterman was about to embark on a
later-to-be-published debate with Albert Ellis and others in the *Journal of Mental
Health Counseling* about social constructionism and postmodernism. The
Guterman–Ellis debate led to related workshops at some of the American Counseling Association's annual conventions in the 1990s. I had the pleasure of
participating in some of these workshops with Guterman and Ellis, along with
other leaders in the field, including Michael D'Andrea, Don C. Locke, and
Sandra A. Rigazio-DiGilio. At times, these workshops were controversial; at
other times, they were especially rewarding as I saw Ellis develop a broader
understanding of development and multiculturalism. Throughout the process,
Guterman played an instrumental role in promoting constructive dialogues in
our field. He has certainly led me to a new respect for Ellis's willingness to
grow and change—something that I also see in Guterman.

For over a decade, Guterman has explicated his solution-focused counseling model
in professional journals and workshops. Building on Steve de Shazer's pioneering
work, Guterman presents a new and exciting model for our field by integrating
solution-focused principles with several themes that are considered defining features
of the counseling profession, including a developmental perspective, an emphasis on
multiculturalism and diversity, and an eclectic approach. I am delighted to see
Guterman's book, *Mastering the Art of Solution-Focused Counseling*, in print because
it presents the principles of solution-focused counseling in comprehensive form. For
counselors who are new to solution-focused counseling, it is an invaluable resource.
For the more experienced counselor, this book provides theoretical discussions, case
examples, and nuances that had not yet been revealed in Guterman's writings.

One of the most basic assumptions informing solution-focused counseling is that clients have existing resources, strengths, and problem-solving skills. If these resources—which solution-focused counselors call *exceptions*—are identified and amplified, then problem resolution and change can be brought about in an effective and efficient manner. This simple idea has powerful implications for counseling. I am reminded, however, that some of the ideas that are considered fundamental to solution-focused counseling are hardly new. Consider, for example, that Leona Tyler (1953) taught us many years ago that our clients have a wide range of capabilities and potentialities. The more I think about it, I have been "solution-focused" for years. The third stage of the five-stage interview focuses on defining client goals, while the postmodern DCT model illustrates multiple approaches to defining goals. Solution-oriented work moves these ideas to the forefront—a point that I now make in a recent version of our microskills text (Ivey & Ivey, 2003). Also, in my DCT, clients are viewed from a developmental, rather than a pathological, perspective.

Focusing on clients' resources is an outgrowth of my own theoretical orientation, originally founded on Tyler's thought and going all the way back to 1966. Positive psychology would also do well to realize that its movement is not new. We all build on the work of others. What *is* new, however, is the original way in which Guterman combines solution-focused elements with principles that are unique to counseling. Guterman presents the material with a curious blend of irreverence and zeal. He frequently reminds us of the limitations of his model. I am also inspired by how he invites readers to bring their own creativity to the mix.

This is a book that shows us how to use positive exceptions to the "problem." I commend this exceptional book by an equally challenging and exceptional author. Keep this book close by your side. It is a valuable resource and a significant contribution to the field.

— *Allen E. Ivey*

PREFACE

It can be said that my journey began before it started. I say this to underscore that everything we do is connected. Solution-focused counseling has been influenced by various clinical models, especially the solution-focused therapy model developed by Steve de Shazer (1985, 1988, 1991, 1994) and his colleagues (de Shazer et al., 1986) at the Brief Family Therapy Center in Milwaukee, Wisconsin. Solution-focused therapy was influenced by the Palo Alto, California based Mental Research Institute's (MRI) interactional therapy (also referred to as communicational/interactional therapy, problem-focused therapy, strategic therapy, MRI, and other variations; Fisch, Weakland, & Segal, 1982; Watzlawick, Weakland, & Fisch, 1974). And the MRI's interactional therapy was influenced by cybernetics (and so forth). If we look at any model, we can trace it back in terms of its influences. So the road that has led me to develop solution-focused counseling has been a shared journey.

A SHARED JOURNEY

A starting point for understanding my journey begins when I was a child. At a young age, I began seeing a psychologist. I was referred to Dr. Daniels because it was determined after some observations by my second-grade teacher that I was unhappy. Back then I was the class clown. But inside I was sad. I don't think Dr. Daniels helped me much. Fortunately, he did not do me harm. Looking back, I suppose he seemed to be psychodynamic.

"Why did you do that?" he would always ask after I would tell him about something I did in class.

"I don't know," I would say.

"There's always a reason," Dr. Daniels would come back.

We never figured out the reason. After 2 years of treatment, Dr. Daniels told my parents that I didn't need to come anymore. And I am thankful for this; it was costing my parents a bundle. As a result of the process, however, I announced to my family and friends at the tender age of 9 that I wanted to be a psychologist when I grew up. It was 1967, and I was in third grade. I offered my services to classmates during recess period. I would actually practice doing psychotherapy with some of my classmates on the playground.

And I am forever grateful to my maternal grandmother, Ida Wolk—my *Nana*—for role-playing as my very first client during her frequent weekend visits.

During my adolescence, my interest in psychology gave way to The Beatles, baseball, and girls. I obtained a bachelor's degree in psychology at Boston University in 1976. But at that time I had no intention of pursuing the field. After graduating, I began working as an assistant manager of a movie theater in Boston. I continued doing this for some time and felt as if my life was aimless. And then a concession attendant working at the theatre asked me a question that changed my life. It was the spring of 1983 and Ellen, a 15-year-old concession attendant—"candy girls" is what we called them—asked me, "Jeff, are you going to be a movie theater manager for the rest of your life?" I don't recall how I responded to her question in the moment. But I pondered her query through the spring of 1983 and realized that I needed to make a change. I needed to do something different.

My parents had moved from New York, where I grew up, to South Florida in 1978 when I was still enrolled at Boston University. In 1983, I called my mother and told her that I was considering enrolling in a master's program in psychology. She was thrilled, and she then suggested I apply to the counseling psychology program at Nova Southeastern University in Fort Lauderdale. I flew to Fort Lauderdale on July 3, 1983, and started taking courses in September.

Despite a near fatal car accident in May 1984, I graduated with a master's in counseling psychology in February 1985. Shortly after graduating, I began working on a psychiatric unit in Fort Lauderdale where I acquired a great deal of clinical experience in a short period of time. Almost immediately, I was required to conduct intakes, individual counseling, and group counseling on a daily basis. My most significant experience at that time occurred when I took a vacation in January 1986. I had a week off and chose to go to New York City. While I was there, I scheduled three personal psychotherapy sessions with rational emotive behavior therapy's (REBT) founder, Albert Ellis. This way I could do a number of things all at once. I could meet the pioneer of the model that I had resonated to during my master's program. I could experience Ellis doing REBT firsthand. And I could also work on some of my personal issues.

My first encounter with Ellis was almost surreal. When I walked into Ellis's office, I found him comfortably reclined in his easy chair waiting for me to arrive. He began our first session by asking, "What problem would you like to start with?" I chose shyness with women. What follows is a verbatim transcript from that first session.

> *Ellis:* What are you telling yourself to *not* approach?
> *Guterman:* I'm not telling myself anything.
> *Ellis:* No. It's never a matter of you not telling yourself anything. You're telling yourself horseshit and then you don't approach. Now what are you telling yourself to not approach?
> *Guterman:* Is that all it comes down to?
> *Ellis:* Yes! It does come down to that.

Guterman: You see, this is strange for me. I came here and I didn't expect this.

Ellis: You didn't expect what?

Guterman: I didn't expect for you to get right to it so quickly. To get to my *B* so quickly.

REBT's ABC theory explains quite simply the processes whereby humans become emotionally and behaviorally disturbed (Ellis, 1991). *A* stands for Activating events. *B* stands for Beliefs. *C* stands for emotional and behavioral Consequences. REBT holds that Activating events (A) do not directly cause emotional and behavioral Consequences (C). Instead, it is one's Beliefs (B) about Activating events (A) that contribute most to emotional and behavioral Consequences (C). REBT's ABC theory posits that appropriate emotional and behavioral Consequences (C) are largely caused by rational Beliefs (B) about Activating events (A). Conversely, inappropriate emotional and behavioral Consequences (C) are mainly caused by irrational Beliefs (B) about Activating events (A).

Ellis: Yeah, because you don't want to deal with it. You're bright, you're attractive, and you're farting around with women. Now, what are you telling yourself to *not* approach? That's the important thing. Are you telling yourself you'll be rejected and be a shit or what?

Guterman: I don't think it's a matter of if I were rejected.

Ellis: Okay. Then if you were *what*? If I approached a woman, *what*? Finish that sentence.

Guterman: I think I feel that I am not good enough.

Ellis: Well, anyone is good enough to try. Even a heathen is good enough to try.

After my sessions with Ellis, I overcame my shyness toward women in social situations and realized that treatment, especially REBT, does work—if you use it! I also learned many of the nuances of REBT by being Ellis's client. Through the years, Ellis's relationship with me evolved from therapist to supervisor to trainer to mentor to colleague (and always friend). Ellis and I went on to participate in a published exchange in the *Journal of Mental Health Counseling (JMHC)* and several workshops at the American Counseling Association's (ACA) annual conventions that contributed to my articulation of solution-focused counseling. Meanwhile, toward the end of the 1980s I continued practicing REBT on the psychiatric unit, and I also began conducting well-attended emotional education workshops at the Broward County public library system in an effort to develop referrals for my small but growing private practice. These workshops resulted in my developing a reputation in the community as an effective REBT counselor. In 1989, however, I chose a new path.

There is an old adage that says, "If the only tool you have is a hammer, you tend to see every problem as a nail." Everywhere I looked, I saw irrational beliefs. And I was good at it. But I wanted to try something different. So when

I heard about the new doctoral program in family therapy at Nova Southeastern University, I became interested. My paternal grandfather had always encouraged me to go for my doctorate. And when I asked Albert Ellis about it, he suggested, "If you intend to remain in the field, then you might as well obtain the highest union card you can get." In September of 1989, I applied to the program.

Just prior to applying to the program, I read an interesting article in the *JMHC* titled "Adding a Systemic Touch to Rational-Emotive Therapy for Families" (T. T. Russell & Morrill, 1989). In this article, the authors proposed an integration of Ellis's REBT and systemic family therapy. I later published two responses to Russell and Morrill's article during my doctoral studies (Guterman, 1991, 1992a), but prior to starting the program, I could only begin to comprehend what the authors were proposing. So I took their article to my admission interview prior to being accepted into the program and brought it to the attention of the faculty. The faculty was hardly receptive to the prospect of an integration of REBT and systemic family therapy. The program was quite cutting edge insofar as it emphasized the narrative and solution-focused models that were so new at the time. I recall one faculty member commenting that attempting such an integration was like trying to combine apples and oranges. I knew little, if anything, at the time about systemic family therapy. Something told me, though, that an apples-and-oranges analogy might be too simple to address the literature that was emerging regarding the feasibility of combining, integrating, or otherwise considering simultaneously REBT and systemic family therapy. But I kept quiet and was respectful of my faculty's insights.

I was not certain of it at the time, but looking back I can now see that when I started the doctoral program I already had the basic idea for my dissertation insofar as it comprised a contrast of REBT and a systemic family therapy model, the MRI's interactional therapy. But I needed a lot of course work and experience in order to get to a place where I could even begin to formulate the research problem. In 1990, I submitted a brief response to T. T. Russell and Morrill's (1989) proposed integration of REBT and systemic family therapy and was surprised when the *JMHC* editor at the time, Lawrence Gerstein, informed me that it was accepted for publication (Guterman, 1991). This was my first scholarly publication, and to this day I will never forget the excitement of being notified that I was being published in a professional journal. I recall that in the 1980s I would read the professional journals, such as the *JMHC* and the *Journal of Counseling & Development*, and I would think to myself, "I want to get published in one of these journals some day!" When I received Lawrence Gerstein's acceptance letter, it became a reality. In 1991, I submitted an expanded response to T. T. Russell and Morrill's (1989) article that was also accepted in the *JMHC* (Guterman, 1992a). This article was a revised and improved version of a qualifying paper—a requirement for my doctoral program—that served as a foundation for my dissertation and, to this day, continues to set forth what I consider to be salient distinctions between REBT's disputation and the reframing method used by many of the systemic family therapy models.

Similar to how Steve de Shazer and his colleagues were influenced by the interactional therapy model developed at the MRI, I was first introduced to the MRI approach during my doctoral studies. Shortly thereafter, I shifted to a solution-focused orientation. Nevertheless, my dissertation (Guterman, 1992b) focused on the interface between REBT and MRI. Although a thorough explication of my dissertation is beyond the scope of this book, it is important to mention briefly here in order to create a context for the ensuing description of my development of solution-focused counseling.

My dissertation showed how Huber and Baruth (1989), in proposing to integrate REBT and MRI in a manner that remains faithful to each approach, had compromised the integrity of each model. A bonus of my work, however, lay in the end product. Following Barbara Held's (1984, 1986, 1991, 1992, 1995) work in the area of the process/content distinction and strategic eclecticism, I showed how one might use REBT theories and techniques within MRI and in such a manner that retains the integrity of MRI (see chapter 3 for a discussion of the theoretical principles of MRI). For now, suffice it to say that like Held, I showed how in some cases, if REBT principles fit with a client's worldview, then the counselor might find REBT to be a fitting metaphor from which to facilitate the goals of MRI. Held's strategic eclecticism has served as a theoretical foundation for the eclectic approach that I later developed for solution-focused counseling.

After getting my doctorate in 1992, I was practicing solution-focused therapy, and I also began considering ways that I might systematically incorporate traditional theories and techniques, especially REBT, within that model. I was betwixt and between, in a liminal stage, and often referred to myself as a "recovering REBT counselor" because while I was trying to follow a straightforward solution-focused approach, I occasionally slipped back to using REBT techniques. I strived to discover a way to justify these REBT "relapses."

In the early 1990s, I was working in a managed care setting, I had a small private practice, and I was teaching in the graduate counseling program at the New York Institute of Technology, Florida Center. In 1993, I also became interested in how social constructionism, an epistemological formulation that has influenced and informed various clinical models, might inform my work. Social constructionism is a theory of knowledge that I understood to be in keeping with the vision of counseling. Basically, social constructionism asserts that knowledge is not an objective representation of nature but, rather, a linguistic creation that arises in the domain of social interchange (Berger & Luckmann, 1967; Gergen, 1985). In 1994, my article, "A Social Constructionist Position for Mental Health Counseling," set forth social constructionism as an epistemological lens from which to clarify the identity of mental health counseling and thereby distinguish our field from the objectivist assumptions inherent in the clinical theories of other disciplines (Guterman, 1994). This article described the history of social constructionism and identified various clinical implications that this framework has for counseling. Toward the end of that article, I suggested that "it is worth considering precisely how social constructionism would inform the 'doing' of . . . [counseling]" (p. 240). This created an impetus for my article, "*Doing* Mental Health Counseling: A Social Constructionist Re-Vision" (Guterman, 1996a), in which I explicated for the first time the solution-focused counseling model. This article included the theoretical basis for strategic eclecticism. It offered a systematic rationale from which to use the theories and techniques from any clinical model—including REBT—within solution-focused counseling.

At this time, I think it is important for me to point out that it is no accident that I make frequent mentions of REBT and Albert Ellis throughout this book. How could I not? The numerous case examples, anecdotes, and references to Ellis and his model are purposeful. Ellis was my first mentor. REBT was my first model. And although I have moved away from REBT, I still find it to be useful at times. Independent of my own leanings, Ellis is arguably the most prominent living psychotherapist in the world. Consider, for example, that Ellis was ranked the second most influential psychotherapist (behind Carl Rogers) in an American Psychological Survey and, further, was found to be the most cited author of works published since 1957 (Smith, 1982).

THE POSTMODERN DEBATE

In 1994, I sent a copy of my article "A Social Constructionist Position for Mental Health Counseling" (Guterman, 1994) to Albert Ellis. My intent was merely to seek personal feedback from Ellis. Little did I know that he would submit a reply to the *JMHC* that instigated a published exchange between numerous writers over the course of the next decade and live workshops at the ACA's annual conventions. The opportunity to debate and exchange ideas—in print and on stage—with leaders in counseling such as Albert Ellis, Allen E. Ivey, Sandra A. Rigazio-DiGilio, Don C. Locke, Michael D'Andrea, Derald Wing Sue, Earl Ginter, and others was one of the highlights of my career. The numerous details of this postmodern debate is beyond the scope of this book, so I refer readers to this large body of work (D'Andrea, 2000; Ellis, 1996b, 1996c, 1997a, 1997b, 2000; Ginter, 1997; Ginter et al., 1996; Guterman, 1994, 1996a, 1996b, 1996c; Guterman et al., 1997; Ivey, Locke, & Rigazio-DiGilio, 1996; Rigazio-DiGilio, 2001; Rigazio-DiGilio, Ellis, D'Andrea, Guterman, & Ivey, 1999; Rigazio-DiGilio, Ivey, & Locke, 1997). But let me share a few of my experiences from this exchange that were memorable for me and served to shape my thinking about counseling and solution-focused counseling.

One of my most memorable experiences was what many counselors have come to refer to as Albert Ellis's "Hitler remark" at the ACA's 1996 annual convention in Pittsburgh. After Ellis and I exchanged articles in the *JMHC* regarding the role of social constructionism in counseling (Ellis, 1996c; Guterman, 1994, 1996b), we presented in a debate format in Pittsburgh at the most well-attended workshop at ACA's 1996 annual convention (Ginter et al., 1996). Earl Ginter, then *JMHC*'s editor, chaired the workshop and invited three guests on the panel: Allen E. Ivey, Sandra A. Rigazio-DiGilio, and Don C. Locke.

The workshop was progressing well, but it was unremarkable until the end when Ellis and I were asked to comment on the presentations made by the three guests. Ellis chose to comment on the Yakima Nation Proverb that Allen Ivey had cited during his presentation. Ivey had recited the following Yakima Nation Proverb in an effort to illustrate social constructionism:

> Progression from childhood to maturity
> is the work of the young.
> But it requires the guidance and support
> of the family and society.
> Education of each boy and girl is the
> gradual revelation of a culture.
> When thoughts and actions become
> one with culture,
> maturity is the result and respect is
> the reward.

Referring to Ivey's citation, Ellis then stated,

> The only thing that puzzled me was that Allen Ivey had up on the screen, "When thoughts and actions become one with culture, maturity is the result and respect is the reward." Now the problem is, as Jeffrey Guterman said originally, it's our interpretation of these things. And one interpretation occurred to me immediately: Well, that's great but then the other was Hitlerism! Hitler was a culture and consequently you have to watch it!

About 20 people in the audience of over 500 broke into spontaneous applause in response to Ellis's remark. Then the applause abruptly ceased. A heated and passionate exchange ensued between the presenters and attendees. Ivey, Rigazio-DiGilio, and Locke expressed objection to Ellis's remark. In a response to Ellis in *Counseling Today* that followed the workshop, Ivey et al. (1996) stated,

> The three of us were perplexed by Ellis' comments. Certainly, the Yakima tradition is not about social control. Rather, Native American Indian proverbs serve to teach children holistically....
>
> Our Jewish students have reminded us that any use of the words "Hitler" or "Nazi" out of context trivializes the Holocaust. Words such as "feminazi" or calling an authoritarian teacher "Hitler" are viewed by many people as failing to see the significance of reality....
>
> Pairing the word "Hitler" with a precious Yakima proverb presents us all with a challenge. Although Ellis modified his comments by speaking of the problems of labeling, he never explained why he made this particular pairing of ideas or used that particular language to discuss reality.
>
> The fact that a substantial number of people applauded his words suggest that they, too, might support the ideas and pairing he presented. This, of course, needs further explication. (p. 33)

Let me attempt to explicate. I imagine that a large number of attendees at the workshop understood and agreed with Ellis's remark, but only a small number applauded. As I sat there on the stage as the discussion following Ellis's remark escalated, a few thoughts ran through my mind. One thought was, "What's all the fuss?" One attendee put it very well, and Ellis agreed. That attendee stated that Ellis was simply noting that just because a group of people agree to call something true, it doesn't make it right. Ellis was reminding us of the insanity of Hitler. He was simply heeding a warning. Another thought that ran through my mind was how ironic it seemed that the only two Jewish people on the stage—Ellis and me—were the only ones who did not seem to be bothered by the Hitler metaphor. What impressed me most about Ellis's Hitler remark, however, was the passion that people felt. It occurred to me that so long as people felt something about what was said, then it was a worthwhile endeavor. At the end of the workshop, a woman approached me. She thanked me for the workshop and said, "I just want you to know that for me this workshop was a life-changing experience." That woman's comment meant a lot to me. That day changed my life, too.

The controversy over Ellis's Hitler remark had legs. It was discussed on the Internet via mailing lists and message boards for months to come. And people still ask me about it today. The postmodern workshop series continued in 1999 at the ACA's annual convention in San Diego, and this time it was Albert Ellis who did the changing. During the workshop in San Diego, Sandra Rigazio-DiGilio, Michael D'Andrea, and Allen Ivey had advocated for the role of social reform in counseling. Toward the end of the workshop, Ivey acknowledged the efforts that Ellis had made in his long career in the area of social advocacy, and he asked whether Ellis would specifically add an *S* to REBT to put a name to the emphasis that he places on social context. Ellis said that he would put a great deal of thought to the role of social reform in counseling and agreed to consider reformulating his theory of REBT accordingly. It was astonishing to observe a master of Ellis's stature willing to accommodate an alternative view live on stage. Allen Ivey closed the workshop by way of a tribute to Albert Ellis. Ivey stated, "Let's remember the moment when we saw a great man become even greater." The workshop concluded with the audience giving Ellis a standing ovation.

A bonus of these two experiences at the ACA workshops was that it exemplified the socially constructed nature of reality in dramatic forms. For me, this was quite fitting with the postmodern and solution-focused approach that I had embraced throughout the past decade. Participating in the postmodern debate—both in print and in workshops—had a positive influence on me insofar as I was able to reconsider my positions about counseling and improve my ideas and practices. For example, Ellis has helped me to clarify my thinking about knowledge and reality and thereby endorse a less radical form of social constructionism (cf. Ellis, 1996c; Guterman, 1996b). The result has been a growing body of work in solution-focused counseling, including writings, workshops, and training. What follows is a comprehensive explication of the model to date. A caveat is offered, namely, that the model is just that: *a* model, not *the* model of counseling. It is not a cookbook. Even if its principles, theories, and techniques are followed as described in this book, counselors will inevitably be required to detour from its map at times in everyday clinical practice (cf. W. H. O'Hanlon & Weiner-Davis, 1989). If anything, I hope readers will take what they find to be useful from this book in hopes that it will embellish their work.

ACKNOWLEDGMENTS

I wish to acknowledge my first mentor, Albert Ellis. I also wish to acknowledge the pioneering solution-focused work of Steve de Shazer and Insoo Kim Berg at the Brief Family Therapy Center in Milwaukee, Wisconsin. I am grateful to my colleagues in the Counseling Department of the Adrian Dominican School of Education at Barry University. The following people offered helpful comments as this book developed: Dale Bertram, Maureen Duffy, Sylvia Fernandez, Allan Jacob, David Kopp, and Noelia Leite. I am especially grateful to Ronald J. Chenail for his extensive review of the book manuscript. Appreciation goes to the American Counseling Association's Director of Publications, Carolyn C. Baker, for her editorial assistance and support. I wish to honor a collaborator, James Rudes, who has contributed significantly to my thinking about counseling. Lastly, I thank my family—my father Robert, my mother Joyce, my sister Lori, my son Julian, and my wife Veronica.

ABOUT THE AUTHOR

Jeffrey T. Guterman, PhD, is an assistant professor of counseling in the Adrian Dominican School of Education at Barry University in Miami Shores, Florida. Originally trained in rational emotive behavior therapy, Dr. Guterman shifted to a solution-focused approach in the early 1990s. Since then, he has been a major contributor to solution-focused counseling. He is the author or co-author of numerous publications. In the past 20 years, he has conducted workshops for professionals, students, and the general public. Dr. Guterman is a licensed mental health counselor in Florida and maintains an active counseling practice, including consultation, training, and supervision. He resides in Miami Beach, Florida. For more information and to contact Dr. Guterman, visit his Web site at http://www.jeffreyguterman.com.

CHAPTER 1
Introduction

This book is about a unique clinical model called *solution-focused counseling*. The model developed from a movement that has produced numerous similar and related treatment approaches such as solution-focused therapy, solution-oriented therapy, strength-based therapy, and competence-based therapy. The solution-focused trend has surely found its place in counseling and psychotherapy. By shifting the focus from problems to solutions, it has rescued many a burned-out counselor. It has been a breath of fresh air for a field that has been stymied by a host of long-term, pathologizing models. And it has found a niche in managed care due to its quick and effective results.

In recent years, solution-focused principles have been applied to a variety of clinical problems and issues, including depression (Johnson & Miller, 1994), domestic violence (Lipchik & Kubicki, 1996), migraine headache (Guterman, Mecias, & Ainbinder, 2005), spirituality and religion (Guterman & Leite, in press), and substance abuse (Berg & Miller, 1992). In addition, this approach has been adapted to various clinical populations and settings, including elderly people (Dahl, Bathel, & Carreon, 2000), schools (Murphy, 1997), and couples and families (Hoyt, 2002). In recent years, a growing body of outcome research has also begun to support the effectiveness of solution-focused approaches to treatment (Cottrell & Boston, 2002; Gingerich & Eisengart, 2000; Pote, Stratton, Cottrell, Shapiro, & Boston, 2003). These and other contributions have resulted in a growing body of knowledge in solution-focused theory, research, and practice that has served to transform a large segment of the profession.

The experiences that contribute to significant transformations of counselors can take many forms. After practicing REBT for almost a decade in the 1980s, I experienced such a shift at about the same time when I read *In Search of Solutions: A New Direction in Psychotherapy* (W. H. O'Hanlon & Weiner-Davis, 1989), a book that describes the theory and practice of solution-focused therapy. For me, it was a change that took place on many levels. In particular, it was a change from a focus on problems and what was not working for my clients to a focus on solutions and what was going right. The following case, which occurred in my practice at about this time, coincided with my transformation.

> For the past 2 months, I had been using an REBT approach with a client named Jon for various problems, including depression, anxiety, and conflicts with coworkers. Then Jon came to a session and reported, "It was a good week." Rather than using REBT (e.g., inquiring about the client's irrational beliefs), I followed up on Jon's statement, "It was a good week." I asked Jon, "What was good about this past week?" Jon described a number of positive events that had occurred, some of which related to his presenting problems and some of which did not. We spoke nothing of REBT or irrational beliefs and only of what was better in his life. I was doing solution-focused therapy.

My shift to a solution-focused approach only occurred after taking a personal and professional journey of sorts (see the Preface). During my master's program in counseling psychology in the early 1980s, I resonated to REBT because none of the other models I was introduced to at the time—psychodynamic, person-centered, gestalt, or behavioral—seemed to fit. And when I took my first position as a mental health counselor on a psychiatric unit in Fort Lauderdale, Florida, in 1985, I became rather proficient at using this model. By 1989, however, I began to feel uneasy about my career path. I began to consider that there might be alternative and more effective ways of conceptualizing problems and change. So, in 1989, I entered the doctoral program in family therapy at Nova Southeastern University. It is worth mentioning here that although I obtained a doctorate in family therapy, I am a licensed mental health counselor and continue to identity myself with the counseling profession. As I show in due course, the model that I subsequently developed is informed by theories in the field of family therapy and other disciplines, yet solution-focused counseling serves to crystallize the unique identity of counseling.

When I finished my doctoral studies in 1992, I made the shift from REBT to solution-focused therapy. And in the next 10 years, I developed my own unique model of solution-focused counseling. This model developed from my clinical experiences, including my work in private practice, managed care, hospitals, community mental health centers, and university counseling centers, and my roles as a counselor, theorist, researcher, trainer, and supervisor. In the past decade, I have also done a great deal of writing and presented numerous workshops and training programs that have contributed to the evolution of solution-focused counseling. Solution-focused counseling, as it has evolved, comprises an integration of solution-focused theories and techniques, an emphasis on postmodern principles, and a strategic approach to eclecticism.

Some readers might wonder if we really need another book that describes a solution-focused clinical model. A unique feature of this book is that it explicates a model unique for the field of counseling insofar as it serves to crystallize our profession's identity and missions, including an emphasis on eclecticism, the client-counselor-relationship, postmodernism, multiculturalism and diversity, and a developmental perspective. In particular, solution-focused counseling's strategic approach to eclecticism allows for the systematic, compatible, and effective application of diverse theories and technique within its model. By virtue of its strategic eclecticism, the model also allows counselors to tailor treatment to account for the uniqueness of each client, apply a variety of interventions, and thereby foster a collaborative approach. Although I have moved away from REBT, I have also come to recognize that it has utility like other traditional theories of counseling and psychotherapy. Accordingly, I have developed a theoretical basis from which to incorporate these clinical theories and techniques within solution-focused counseling and, moreover, in a manner that retains the integrity of my model.

Solution-focused counseling has been described in numerous articles (e.g., Guterman, 1996a, 1996b, 1996c, 1998; Guterman & Leite, in press; Guterman et al., 2005; Rudes & Guterman, 2005) and has been presented in many workshops and training programs. I have taught its principles, theories, and techniques in many graduate courses. But to date there is no thorough explication of the model in book form. I have frequently received requests from counselors, colleagues, and students for just such a resource. Up until now, all I could say was, "I am working on it." In this book, I explicate a comprehensive description of the theory, practice, and various applications of the model. My aim in this book is to address both the complex theoretical underpinnings that inform solution-focused counseling and its numerous practice strategies in a simple and straightforward language so that it is accessible to counselors who wish to incorporate this framework in their work. In this first chapter, I identify and describe the fundamental principles that inform solution-focused counseling. I conclude this chapter with a brief description of the organization of the book.

PRINCIPLES OF SOLUTION-FOCUSED COUNSELING

I now identify and describe some of the fundamental principles of solution-focused counseling in hopes of establishing a foundation for understanding the model. These principles include (a) solution focus; (b) collaborative approach; (c) small changes can lead to big results; (d) emphasis on process; (e) strategic approach to eclecticism; (f) brief by design, but not always; and (g) responsiveness to multiculturalism and diversity.

Solution Focus

Solution-focused counseling, like other counseling models, is not value free. It operates in keeping with a view of what problems are and what problems are not. Solution-focused counseling holds that people have existing strengths, resources, and problem-solving skills—in effect, the natural resources that are needed to solve the problems that bring them to counseling. Accordingly, the emphasis in this approach is to focus on what is working in clients' lives, rather than on what is not working. This approach stands in stark contrast to the prevailing and traditional models of counseling that tend to be problem-focused and attempt to reexplain the client's problem in terms of elaborate theories of problem formation and change processes.

I now view people like bicycle chains (cf. W. H. O'Hanlon & Wilk, 1987). Basically, they work very simply and well. Sometimes they get a bit stuck or off track, and in such cases they might need a minor adjustment. In such cases, if I become too involved in defining the problem or contributing to making a change, then I run the risk of exacerbating the problem or becoming part of it. My task, as I see it, is to get in and out quickly and let the client be on his or her way with a minimum of intervention. As I see it, counseling ought to be like brain surgery. The counselor should get in and out quickly without the client hardly knowing that the counselor was ever there. This way, the client can more easily get back on track. When you understand solution-focused principles, then a wellness perspective become a logical consequence.

Collaborative Approach

Solution-focused counseling is informed by postmodernism and, in particular, a social constructionist epistemological framework that holds that reality is cocreated in conversations between people. Accordingly, problems are conceptualized as the language, talk, or conversations that transpire between clients and counselors. In other words, counselors and clients collaborate to define the presenting problems and goals in treatment. In contrast, modernist models of counseling take an educative and authoritative approach in which theories, techniques, and goals of treatment tend to be imposed on the client.

Postmodernism, as I describe in chapter 2, holds that a single, stable, and fixed notion of reality is dubious. Hence, it is questionable for the counselor to impose the "correct" notion of what is or is not a problem, or what the goal shall be. What might be a problem to one client might not be a problem to another (and vice versa). At the same time, I recognize that I am an active participant in the counseling process, and therefore I cannot *not* influence my client in some regard. So, inevitably, the process of defining problems and goals is a collaborative process of negotiation between the client and me. In most cases, however, I agree to work on what my client considers to be the problem and goal.

Small Changes Can Lead to Big Results

Frequently, a small change is all that is needed to resolve the problems that bring clients to counseling. And a small change can also result in a snowball effect that, in turn, leads to bigger changes and the resolution of bigger problems that might face clients. This idea is closely linked to the principle of inertia, which holds that an object at rest tends to stay at rest and an object in motion tends to stay in motion. Consider how difficult it is for some clients who procrastinate doing some arduous task such as laundry, paying bills, school work, and so forth. Inertia principles suggest that it takes an extra force of energy to initially propel the body into motion to start the task. Once a person initiates the activity, that is, when they make the small albeit significant effort, then this often leads to progress. The person often finds it easier to stay in motion and proceed with the activity.

Taking the first step is nontrivial as it often takes an extra effort, a sudden burst of activity. And I frequently look to my clients to uncover the how of these exceptional events as these hold the key to their problem-solving capabilities and skills. It also holds true that when it comes to human relationships, a small change in one part of the system often leads to changes in other parts of the system. Accordingly, if a spouse does something a little different in his or her interactions with his or her partner, then it is likely that the partner will respond slightly differently which, in turn, will result in changes in the nature of the relationship.

Emphasis on Process

A distinguishing feature of solution-focused counseling is its emphasis on change processes, rather than content to be changed. It follows that it is our job as counselors to focus on identifying and amplifying the exceptions to clients' problems rather than focus on the problems themselves. Hence, the focus is on process, not content. It follows that it is neither necessary nor is it preferable to obtain extensive historical information or know the cause of the problem to create a solution. It is granted that if you take your car to a repair shop, you need to know the cause of the problem to fix it. But this does not seem to always apply to human affairs. It appears, then, that in solution-focused counseling, our clients are usually the experts of the content to be changed, whereas we are experts of change processes. Again, our job is to point clients in the direction of change, not to tell them what to change.

Strategic Approach to Eclecticism

As just mentioned, it is not necessary to know a lot about the problem in order to solve it. Some clients, however, believe in a search for causes to their problems. In such cases, I join my clients in the search. A strategic approach to eclecticism allows for such an approach. I assess early on in counseling whether or not my client has bought into the idea that there is some cause and, further, if it is necessary to discover such a cause in order to solve his or her problem. This mindset can become a self-fulfilling prophesy. Clients might have gotten this idea from past counseling experiences, from our culture, or media depictions of counseling. The objective truth of theories of causation in our field is dubious and not the issue at hand. The question is the degree to which clients will act *as if* there is a cause. And in that sense, it is a reality to them. Therefore, I had better take it seriously and buy into it with them. Similar to how I respect the idiosyncratic worldview of my client and use it during the change process, I do the same if his or her view corresponds to a theory from some other counseling model. Because I am a participant in the counseling process, there might also be instances when I find that it is fitting to introduce the formal theory from other theoretical systems. This is especially true when clients are in search of a cause but are unable to find one.

Brief by Design, But Not Always

Counselors of various orientations and backgrounds need to be prepared for cases when clients might drop out of treatment or when access to treatment might be limited by insurance companies and third-party payers. It is increasingly important, then, for counselors to develop and demonstrate skills in brief counseling for at least two reasons: (a) to help clients who might drop out of treatment or otherwise discontinue treatment before the counselor's or the client's preferred goals are realized, and (b) to compete as providers for health maintenance organizations (HMOs) and managed behavioral health companies. When clients discontinue counseling before a consensual termination occurs between the client and counselor, this can be described as "brief counseling by default." A brief, focused treatment plan was not necessarily, but might have been, formulated by the counselor or the client, but treatment nevertheless ended in a short period of time. Perhaps the counselor sees the drop out as "premature." Perhaps we need to consider, however, that this assessment might be premature. Maybe some drop-outs happen because the clients think they are better. And maybe they *are* better in significant ways; for example, they have become unstuck, the crisis is over, or they have begun to apply their own natural, effective solutions to whatever brought them to treatment in the first place.

It is likely that most counselors at times use brief counseling techniques. For example, in his book *Better, Deeper, and More Enduring Brief Therapy*, Albert Ellis (1996a) has acknowledged that if and when he finds that his bread-and-butter REBT techniques are ineffective, then he will use solution-focused techniques within his REBT framework. The ensuing change might not necessarily be the elegant change that Ellis prefers (i.e., the disputation of the client's core, irrational belief system), but I would say it is good change, especially if we consider that the alternative might be—no change!

Counseling models that are "brief by design" correspond to theories in which quick results are not flukes but, rather, are natural and expected. The quick results of solution-focused counseling are more a byproduct of its perspective rather than an end in itself. When brief counseling is by design, brevity is the residue of the counselor's perspective. Most clients bring to counseling a readiness for change—a window of opportunity—that might be missed if we do not zero in on, highlight, and amplify these natural, problem-solving mechanisms. It is critical, then, to have an acute and ongoing awareness that each and every counseling session could be the last counseling session. This is not to say that solution-focused counseling is always brief. It is brief by design, but it does not always work out that way. I set out in each session with the understanding that this might be my last session with this client. Therefore, I always try to be focused. Perhaps it would be more fitting, then, to describe the model as focused by design rather than brief by design. I have had some long-term cases. Sometimes I see a client for an extended period, sometimes extending over a number of years. Although this is rare, this happens sometimes. Generally, though, my treatment episodes last from 3 to 10 sessions. If a significant change does not happen in the first or second session, then it is unlikely that I will be of much help to my client.

Responsiveness to Multiculturalism and Diversity

Multiculturalism has been described as a fourth force in counseling (Pedersen, 1990, 1998). In particular, Pedersen (1990) has suggested that we need to get past understanding multiculturalism as merely a specialty in our field and, instead, see it as a framework that informs nothing less than everything we do. Moreover, Pedersen has pointed out that "we have tended to use culture as something that belongs to us rather than a network of relationships to which we ourselves belong" (1990, p. 94). From this perspective, it is to be understood that clients and counselors ideally teach and learn from one another and thereby cocreate cultures of counseling.

In solution-focused counseling, multiculturalism is broadly defined to address various domains, including gender, sexual orientation, disability, ethnicity, race, socioeconomic status, age, spirituality, religion, and family structure. Solution-focused counseling recognizes the importance of developing self-awareness, acquiring knowledge, and building skills relevant to the diverse worldviews of clients (Lee, 2001). It is also important for solution-focused counselors to gain an understanding of how the diverse worldviews of clients inform, influence, and have an impact on problems and solutions. From a multicultural perspective, each and every clinical case sets the stage for the cocreation of a new theory of counseling. It follows that solution-focused counselors strive to learn about the collective worldviews of many diverse cultural groups and, also, the idiosyncratic viewpoints of the individuals that make up these groups. Furthermore, solution-focused counselors recognize that their own worldviews necessarily influence clients and therefore make every effort to do so in ways that contribute to the cocreation of constructive therapeutic dialogues and change.

ORGANIZATION OF THIS BOOK

Having described the basic principles of solution-focused counseling, it is now possible for me to describe the ensuing organization of the rest of the book.

Chapters 2 and 3 address the theoretical underpinnings of solution-focused counseling. In chapter 2, I describe the postmodern epistemological formulation that informs the model. In this chapter, I briefly trace the history and role of epistemology in the field of counseling and psychotherapy, including the shift from modernism to postmodernism. In particular, I examine the roles that constructivism and social constructionism have played in informing solution-focused counseling. In chapter 3, the theory of problem formation and change in solution-focused counseling is presented. This chapter also includes an explication of the strategic approach to eclecticism used within solution-focused counseling.

In chapters 4, 5, and 6, I describe the clinical process of solution-focused counseling. In chapter 4, "Before the First Session," the phenomenon of pretreatment change is introduced. In this chapter, it is suggested that positive changes often occur before clients come to the first session. An increasing literature has documented research on this phenomenon called *pretreatment change.* I have made pretreatment change a hallmark of solution-focused counseling by making a point of contacting clients by telephone before they come in for the first session. This chapter provides details for how counselors can help clients build on and amplify the positive changes that occur before formal counseling begins and thereby enhance treatment. In chapter 5, "The First Session," the clinical process used during the first session is described, including coconstructing a problem and goal, identifying and amplifying exceptions, and coconstructing tasks. In chapter 6, "After the First Session," I address various clinical issues that arise following the first session, including identifying and amplifying exceptions derived from tasks and terminating counseling.

In chapters 7, 8, 9, and 10, clinical applications of solution-focused counseling are provided. In chapter 7, a solution-focused application to depression is described. In chapter 8, a solution-focused approach to substance problems is provided. In chapter 9, the application of solution-focused counseling to various problems and client populations are described. In chapter 10, "Jared's Complaint," an extensive case example is provided.

Finally, the book concludes with chapter 11, "The Future of Solution-Focused Counseling," in which new directions for solution-focused counseling are considered.

CHAPTER 2

A Postmodern Perspective

The purpose of this chapter is to consider postmodernism as an epistemological foundation for solution-focused counseling. Perhaps no other topic has created as much debate and confusion in the domain of philosophy and our field as epistemology. Much of the confusion has been the result of the failure to define the term *epistemology* and related terms clearly and consistently. So I attempt here to address this complex, yet very important, topic in as simple and straightforward a manner as possible.

Put simply, *epistemology* is defined as a branch of philosophy that studies knowledge. Epistemology asks the question, "What is knowledge?" or "How do we know what we know?" This is to be contrasted with the domain of *ontology,* which refers to the study of being or the study of reality. Thus, ontology is concerned with the study of what is known, whereas epistemology studies the processes of knowing itself. An epistemologist might ask, then, "Is it possible to attain objective (i.e., independent of the observer) truth or is knowledge the result of my own (i.e., subjective) creation?"

Epistemological assumptions lie at the core of virtually all clinical theories. The majority of traditional clinical models have been informed by empiricist, positivist, rationalist, or realist epistemologies (hereafter also referred to as modernist epistemologies) that contend that it is possible to attain or approximate objective knowledge of reality (Held, 1990, 1991). I posit that, on one hand, a modernist epistemological view lies at the core of these disciplines' reductionistic and, hence, pathologizing clinical theories. The theory and practice of solution-focused counseling, on the other hand, is informed by a postmodern epistemological view which holds that knowledge is a subjective phenomenon.

Consider, for example, that Sigmund Freud was a proponent of logical positivism, an epistemological view that corresponds to the modernist school (Gay, 1988). Psychoanalysis was and, to some degree, still is considered a true science of the psyche. Freud developed his clinical model as a branch of medicine. In Freud's lifetime it was almost impossible to be accepted into a psychoanalytic

9

institute without a medical degree. In some circles, psychology remains a scientific discipline that endeavors to apply empirical and scientific methods in order to discover truth claims. Although many of the mainstream theorists and clinical models in our field have recently endorsed postmodern ideas, a closer examination of their clinical theories and practices suggests that they continue to conceptualize problems and change in keeping with modernist conceptions. Solution-focused counseling and other postmodern clinical models, therefore, are to be considered more in terms of narrative, rather than scientific, disciplines. Given solution-focused counseling's emphasis on language, it might also be more fitting to associate solution-focused counseling with literary disciplines such as rhetoric, linguistics, and hermeneutics and therefore place it in a conversational domain. It follows that solution-focused counseling is to be considered more of an art than a science.

Before I describe the development of postmodernism and the clinical implications of this framework for solution-focused counseling, let me propose that it is not a necessary requirement for counselors to address epistemological and other complex philosophical issues let alone resolve them in order to be effective in their clinical work. Held and Pols (1985) have suggested, however, that if counselors choose to consider these issues, then they had better do so intelligently and with rigor. Indeed, many of the debates and confusions regarding epistemology remain unsettled in our field and in philosophy. I have not addressed these debates and confusions as doing so would be extraneous to the present discussion.

POSTMODERNISM

Postmodernism is a relative term. And this seems fitting given that in many circles, including counseling, postmodernism corresponds to a reaction against modernist conceptions of certainty, truth, and objectivity. Postmodernism has influenced various fields, including art, literature, anthropology, politics, economics, and philosophy. In each case, these fields have embraced the postmodern idea that knowing is a subjective phenomenon. Although there are various factions of postmodern thought, these theories share the view that there are limits to human knowledge. As Walter Truett Anderson (1990) has suggested, in the postmodern world, reality isn't what it used to be.

Constructivism and social constructionism have emerged as among the most influential postmodern theories in counseling and psychotherapy. In developing solution-focused counseling, I have embraced a social constructionist perspective because I consider it to be a theory of knowledge that is more in keeping with the vision of counseling and one that serves to clarify the assumptions that distinguishes counseling from other disciplines. Social constructionism asserts that knowledge is not an objective representation of nature but, rather, a linguistic creation that arises in the domain of social interchange (Berger & Luckmann, 1967; Gergen, 1985). This epistemological doctrine has surfaced from constructivism, which holds that knowledge is the result of our own (i.e., subjective) cognitive processes. It follows that social constructionism and constructivism conceptualize knowledge at the social and biological levels, respectively. I have adopted a social constructionist framework for solution-focused counseling because it rejects pathologizing conceptualizations of clients and, like counseling's vision (Ginter, 1989a, 1989b; Ivey, 1989), considers the client–counselor relationship integral to the change process (H. Anderson & Goolishian, 1988; Hoffman, 1990; M. White & Epston, 1990). A closer examination of social constructionism also reveals clinical implications that are in keeping with counseling's developmental perspective (Ivey, 1989, 2000). Although I favor social constructionism, there is also value in the constructivist view. Accordingly, prior to discussing the development of social constructionism, I briefly describe the development of constructivism and how this epistemological movement has influenced the field of counseling and psychotherapy.

Constructivism

The emergence of social constructionism was preceded by the development of constructivism, which was founded in the European traditions of Kant (1929), Vico (1948), Berkeley (1963), Schopenhauer (1907), Wittgenstein (1963), Vaihinger (1924), and Piaget (1954). It has been suggested that constructivism and social constructionism are synonymous (e.g., Held, 1990). A closer look at these epistemological formulations, however, suggests otherwise (Guterman, 1994; Hoffman, 1990).

Constructivism holds that knowledge is not an objective reflection of reality but, rather, is the result of our own (i.e., subjective) cognitive processes (Watzlawick, 1984). Versions of constructivism have been described in various disciplines, including cognitive science (Varela, 1979), biology (Maturana & Varela, 1988), and cybernetics (von Foerster, 1984). For example, Maturana has set forth a biologically based theory of constructivism through experiments on the color vision of frogs (Maturana & Varela, 1988). Maturana showed that the frog's brain does not process images as a camera does. Instead, frogs transform images like music on compact discs (Guterman, 1994; Hoffman, 1990). This has led to the understanding that social interaction occurs between informationally closed systems (Maturana & Varela, 1988). On the basis of this view, Hoffman (1990) has described the constructivist formulation as one that places people in biological isolation booths.

In my graduate classes, I often conduct a simple exercise to exemplify constructivism. I begin by asking and stating the following: "By a show of hands, who in the class thinks that they see me? Raise your hand if you see me right now." I get different reactions to this exercise. Usually, though, a majority of the students raise their hands. It is hard to argue that one does not see me. I might ask the students who did not raise their hands to support their views. Or I might ask the students who raised their hands to defend their perspectives. And then we engage in an epistemological debate. In each case, however, I try to show my students that the image of "me" actually resides in their brains. I acknowledge that I am not a biologist but, nevertheless, briefly describe the process whereby light hits the eye and is converted into an image that resides within the boundaries of the organism. This logic is hard to refute, and I seldom, if ever, am challenged. So I quickly have a group of converted constructivists on my hands. I then go on to suggest that all of our experiences—sight, smell, hearing, feeling, and so forth—are the result of our subjective and active constructing processes.

This is not to say that constructivism is not open to criticism. Consider, for example, that Albert Ellis (1996c) has reminded us of philosopher Bertrand Russell (1950), who "once sagely remarked, anyone who thinks that human happiness and survival solely comes from within had better be condemned to spend a night in a raging storm in subzero weather, wearing rags!" (p. 20). Let me respond to Ellis's point by saying that I do not think that human constructions are *purely* subjective or that we are not influenced by reality. The influences of nature are real, and moreover, we interact with (and thereby both influence and are influenced by) the environment. From a biologically based constructivist perspective, I argue, however, that although subzero weather influences the knower, the pain resides within the boundaries of the organism. This does not make the pain any less real. The question at hand is, Where is the pain located? There are three principal factors to consider regarding the relationship between knowledge and reality: location, location—and *location*!

If we accept the constructivist theory that individuals construct their own subjective realities, then counselors have an ethical imperative to recognize that there are potentially multiple clinical realities. This has led to the emergence of various clinical models named to denote this trend, including "constructivist therapy" or "constructivist counseling." Constructivism has also provided a rationale for the use of reframing, a cognitive-change technique that has emerged in the last quarter century as an alternative to traditional cognitive restructuring (Guterman, 1992a). Cognitive restructuring involves helping clients modify through scientific methods the irrational beliefs, cognitive distortions, and antiempirical inferences that are presumed to be etiologically related to emotional disturbances. Reframing, however, is designed to help clients ascribe alternative, equally valid meanings to situations and thereby enact more effective problem-solving strategies. It can be seen, then, that different methods of justification are generally used for cognitive restructuring and reframing. The former uses scientific methods that correspond to a modernist framework. The latter uses the client's subjective worldview—his or her own constructions—as a basis from which to reframe events and effect a change in behavior (Guterman, 1992a).

Social Constructionism

Allen Ivey (1989) has suggested that the identity of counseling can be clarified by adopting the constructivist–developmental perspective that has been set forth in counseling circles (e.g., Guidano, 1987; Joyce-Moniz, 1985; Mahoney, 1985).

A review of the works by Guidano (1987), Joyce-Moniz (1985), and Mahoney (1985) suggests that these models are informed by the biologically based constructivism just described. I have found, however, that social constructionism is more congruent with counseling's developmental approach and, moreover, counseling's focus on the client–counselor relationship. For example, although both constructivism and social constructionism endorse a subjectivist view of knowledge, the former emphasizes individuals' biological and cognitive processes, whereas the latter places knowledge in the domain of social interchange. As de Shazer (1991) has noted, although constructivism emphasizes subjectivity, "it seems to draw . . . the methodological boundary around the client, who is the individual cognizing subject" (pp. 46–47).

In contrast with constructivism's European beginnings, social constructionism was developed mainly in the United States in various disciplines, including literary theory (Culler, 1982; Genette, 1980; Lakoff & Johnson, 1980), anthropology (Geertz, 1973), and social psychology (Berger & Luckmann, 1967; Gergen, 1985; G. Kelly, 1955). Unlike constructivism, which holds that that human knowledge is biologically based, social constructionism contends that ideas are located in the domain of language between persons. Hoffman (1990) has stated that "as we move through the world, we build up our ideas about it in conversation with other people" (p. 3). Similarly, Gergen (1985) has stated that from a social constructionist view, knowledge is the "result of an active, cooperative enterprise of persons in relationship" (p. 267). There are many examples of socially constructed realities in everyday life. Money is a rich example. Independent of the definition that we as a society have ascribed, money has no value. Other examples could fill this book, so I will provide only a few more to make the point.

In 2002, I was amazed at how such a large segment of the United States rallied behind the Bush administration's preemptive invasion of Iraq. It is not my intent here to take sides, pro or con, for the invasion. The point is that on the basis of the information that was presented by the United States government, whether the intelligence was good or bad, a consensus was reached. Then, less than 2 years later, another seeming consensus grew in the United States, namely, that the government should never have gone into Iraq in the first place. There is no objective truth to either side of the argument. I present this historical anecdote only to show where these diametrically opposed views are located: in the hands of people in relationship.

Another socially constructed reality is the *Diagnostic and Statistical Manual of Mental Disorders*, fourth edition, text revision (*DSM–IV–TR*; American Psychiatric Association [APA], 2000). The *DSM–IV–TR* (hereafter also referred to as the *DSM*) is a social artifact (Duffy, Gillig, Tureen, & Ybarra, 2002; Gorman, 2001; Guterman, 1994, 1996b). In a published response to Albert Ellis (1996c), I suggested the following understanding of the *DSM*:

> The *DSM* consists of an elaborate system of if-then criteria that have been socially constructed to ascribe pathologizing labels to clinical phenomena. In effect, any given DSM category is tautological (i.e., circular and

irrefutable) as long as its if-then propositions are upheld (Bateson, 1979). What is all too often forgotten, however, is that its community of stakeholders has created the if-then conditions in the first place. Any so-called truth regarding whether or not such categories exist is made legitimate merely by its community of stakeholders' proclivity to describe clients accordingly. (Guterman, 1996b, pp. 35–36)

Along similar lines, our theories of counseling are to be understood as social constructions. Moreover, various social constructionist clinical models have been developed in recent years (e.g., H. Anderson, 1996; H. Anderson & Goolishian, 1988; Bruner, 1986; de Shazer, 1985, 1988, 1991; Howard, 1991; Mair, 1988; M. White & Epston, 1990). These models share the view that problems are cocreated in social conversation. The change process entails a therapeutic conversation between counselors and clients whereby alternative stories are cocreated. I have previously suggested (Guterman, 1994) that social constructionism holds promise as an organizing framework to address Ginter's (1989a) call for a focus on client–counselor relationship factors and the developmental perspective described by Ivey (1989). In the next section, I describe several clinical implications of a social constructionist position for solution-focused counseling.

CLINICAL IMPLICATIONS

Reality as a Social Construction

Social constructionism recognizes that knowledge is a social invention rather than an objective representation of reality (W. T. Anderson, 1990; Berger & Luckmann, 1967; Gergen, 1985; Hoffman, 1990). This perspective seems to contradict most schools' views of reality, especially those espoused by clinical psychology and psychiatry. The billion-dollar industry of psychiatry, for example, is organized around and invested in the practice of rendering an objective view of the world. Recently, however, some counseling writers have begun to challenge the validity of psychiatric diagnosis and nosology (Ginter, 1989a, 1989b; Guterman, 1994; Ivey, 1989). For example, Ginter (1989a) has stated that "labeling someone always represents some sort of socially embedded process and too often is less 'scientific' than we assume" (p. 341). Ginter (1989a) has also suggested that "the fact that a significant number of 'professionals' are involved in the development and modification of a labeling system does not guarantee that it is generally objective in nature" (p. 340). Watzlawick et al. (1974) have contended that the concept of objective reality so ubiquitous in psychiatry is, itself, a social construction:

> When the concept of reality is referred to in psychiatric discourse, this is rarely the reality of a thing per se, i.e., its basic properties, if such do exist, or even what is simply observable, though this is the ostensible subject. Rather, the "reality" referred to concerns . . . the meaning and value at-

tributed to the phenomenon in question. This is a far cry from the simplistic but widespread assumption that there is an objective reality, somewhere "out there," and that sane people are more aware of it than crazy ones. On reflection it becomes obvious that anything is real only to the extent that it conforms to a definition of reality—and those definitions are legion. To employ a useful oversimplification: real is what a sufficiently large number of people have agreed to call real—except that this fact is usually forgotten; the agreed-on definition is reified (that is, made into a "thing" in its own right) and is eventually experienced as that objective reality "out there" which apparently only a madman [or madwoman] can fail to see. (pp. 96–97)

It follows that social constructionists object to the widespread locution, "The client is out of touch with reality." Along similar lines, a social constructionist would reject the concept of denial because this implies that there exists an objective reality of which the counselor is aware and the client is not (Guterman, 1994). As I have suggested, "from a social constructionist perspective, one could say that we are all out of touch with reality if the reality in question is deemed as existing in an objective sense" (Guterman, 1994, p. 231). In contrast, social constructionists understand that clients and counselors share a reciprocal role in coconstructing clinical "realities" because so-called reality exists in the domain of intersubjective communication. It follows that all clinical theories, including those that correspond to modernist epistemologies, are not objective representations but, rather, are allegories, metaphors—in effect stories—that we create.

Counselors as Participant–Observers

The concept of socially constructed realities sets forth important implications for the client–counselor relationship that Ginter (1989a, 1989b) has suggested are integral to counseling. For example, if we accept that clinical theories are social inventions, it follows that counselors play a participatory role in each and every aspect of theory building, research, and practice. Borrowing from the field of anthropology, some social constructionists have described their role as a participant–observer (e.g., Guterman, 1994; Keeney, 1983) who is inseparably connected to, rather than independent of, their clients. Keeney (1983) has contrasted this understanding with the modernist perspective in which clinicians are viewed as independent of their clients and "act upon the . . . fundamental assumption that they are 'in charge' of creating change, and that they must remain outside the system being treated" (p. 80). Such a view is premised in notions of objectivity and pathology that run counter to a social constructionist position.

My introduction to the concept of participation–observation was through the work of anthropologist Clifford Geertz. In his seminal book, *Interpretation of Cultures*, Geertz (1973) showed that an anthropologist, when studying any given culture, cannot be a fly on the wall. Instead, an anthropologist influences the people that he or she observes and thus both influences and is influenced by the subject under study; hence, he or she is a participant–observer. To illustrate the point, Geertz told a story of two natives in a cave. One of the natives warned the other, "Look, here comes the anthropologist walking our way. Hurry and put away the transistor radio." Geertz taught us that anthropologists do not study villages, they study *in* villages.

As counselors, we cannot *not* influence our clients. Give up the idea of neutrality. But we do have choices. We can choose how we conceptualize problems and change and the methods from which to help clients solve their problems. Viewing ourselves as participant–observers is nontrivial when we consider Keeney's (1983) point that "descriptions of clients who are institutionalized, have electrical voltage charged through their brains, or have drugs pumped into their veins give us information about their therapists" (p. 81). One could even argue that a counselor's diagnosis says more about the counselor than the client who is being diagnosed. A social constructionist position contends that when a counselor describes clients in terms of pathological categories, this indicates that he or she has conversed within the context of a professional community that, in turn, has chosen to organize its knowledge accordingly.

Don't get me wrong. I recognize that the *DSM* and psychiatric nosology is entrenched in our culture (Guterman, 1996b, 2005). We need the *DSM* to justify reimbursement from health insurance companies. In addition, counselors who do not use the *DSM* are at risk for falling below community standards of care. Accordingly, my solution-focused counseling approach involves conducting a formal intake, including a comprehensive psychosocial history, a thorough mental status examination, formulating a multiaxial diagnostic impression, and making psychiatric referrals for clients who meet the criteria for certain diagnoses (e.g., major depression, bipolar disorder, and schizophrenia). When I complete the intake, however, I proceed to coconstruct a problem with the client in keeping with a solution-focused approach to counseling.

Ginter (1989a) has suggested that we "use what occurs between counselor and client as one of the pillars of mental health counseling, using it as a focal point for theory development" (p. 342). Understanding counselors as participant-observers may help us examine the client–counselor relationship in counseling more relevantly. Social constructionists explicitly recognize the connection of the observer with the observed (Keeney, 1983). This recognition, in turn, leads social constructionists to consider several critical ethical imperatives. In particular, social constructionist models set forth the ethical imperative to recognize the participatory role that counselors play in the change process and to discern the client–counselor relationship as the locus of change (Guterman, 1994).

Language-Determined Systems

It is reaffirmed that counselors operating in keeping with social constructionism—like those who embrace the modernist epistemologies—necessarily impose their

Mastering the Art of Solution-Focused Counseling

own (i.e., subjective) theories in the clinical process. As Liddle (1982) has suggested, "One cannot not have a theory" (p. 244). Ginter (1988) has similarly suggested that "therapy cannot exist without theory" (p. 3). To avoid ascribing clinical theories is thus an impossibility. The issue at hand concerns how we choose to do so.

Traditionally, the fields of clinical psychology, psychiatry, social work, family therapy, and counseling have viewed problems as the result of some objectively defined social system, whether that system was an individual, couple, family, legal domain, professional community, or society. H. Anderson, Goolishian, Pulliam, and Winderman (1986) have stated that "although the various therapies disagree on which is the appropriate social structure to consider when doing therapy, they all share the common belief that one or the other of the various social structures is the prime locus or cause of problems" (p. 117). Psychiatry and clinical psychology each tend to locate problems within the individual. Many of the family therapies, however, in an attempt at moving away from pathologizing the individual, have shifted the pathologizing focus to the family system as a whole. H. Anderson and Goolishian (1988) have described this perspective as one that locates problems in a social system:

> In this prevailing view . . . human systems are seen as sociocultural systems organized according to role and structure, and as characterized by stability, hierarchy, power, and control. That is, sociocultural systems are defined and maintained by social organization through social role and social structure. (pp. 375–376)

In contrast, social constructionists have reconceptualized problems and have redefined the phenomena otherwise associated with pathological human systems. Accordingly, the concept *problem-determined systems* has been developed to account for the assumption that human systems (e.g., individuals, couples, and families) do not create problems, but, rather, social communication, interchange, and language about problems creates systems (H. Anderson & Goolishian, 1988; H. Anderson et al., 1986; Hoffman, 1990). In other words, problems are not the result of an objective defect that exists within or between individuals, but, rather, "the distinction of the system of treatment concern . . . is defined by those who share in the communication that defines a problem" (H. Anderson et al., 1986, p. 118). In other words, the problem creates the system rather than the system creates the problem (Hoffman, 1990).

It could be argued that despite their problem-determined systems perspective, social constructionists run the risk of shifting the pathologizing focus from human systems to the language itself that theoretically creates problems. For example, Howard (1991) has described social constructionist psychotherapy as involving "story repair," as if clients' narratives are defective in an objective sense. This is a particular concern for counseling when considering that from a developmental perspective, clients' clinical presentations are not to be viewed as pathological but, rather, as challenges, life transitions, and opportunities for growth (Ivey, 1989, 2000). Accordingly, I favor the term *language-determined systems* or *language systems* (H. Anderson & Goolishian, 1988; Epstein & Loos, 1989) over problem-determined systems when conceptualizing clinical presentations: The former term captures the meaning intended from both a social constructionist and a developmental orientation insofar as it averts imposing notions of pathology.

Ivey (1989) has taken a position in keeping with a language systems perspective by suggesting that within a developmental approach to counseling, "distinctions between pathology and normality become irrelevant" (p. 29). Ivey's point raises questions, however, regarding whether the confusion and concern regarding the professional identity of counseling has been reinforced, in part, by the title *mental health counselor* because it begs the other side of the distinction, thereby suggesting that we are also "mental illness counselors." Perhaps, then, it would be more fitting for us to refer to ourselves as "language systems counselors."

From a language-determined systems perspective, there are no clinical problems in the world per se. In other words, clinical problems do not exist in any objective sense (i.e., independent of the conversations that occur between clients and counselors). Herein lies a foundational premise of a social constructionist approach and one that addresses Ginter's (1989a, 1989b) call for a more focused examination of client–counselor relationship factors. If we accept that counselors are participant–observers, then it follows that when we participate in any given clinical process whereby communications define treatment concerns, we have necessarily become part of that language system. Hence, the essence of counseling is an interpersonal process between counselors and clients whereby problems and goals are cocreated.

A Collaborative Approach

In keeping with the concepts of participant–observation and language systems just described, the social constructionist approach in solution-focused counseling takes a collaborative position with clients in contrast to the educative stance that is usually assumed within the context of modernist models. This emphasis has been occasioned by a progressive reconceptualization of the concept of resistance within social constructionist circles.

Resistance has been a time-honored conception in the fields of counseling and psychotherapy. Since the beginnings of psychoanalysis over a century ago, resistance has traditionally been defined as clients' oppositions to the changes that have been prescribed by the clinician. In clinical psychology, for example, it has been theorized that resistance is usually the result of individual pathological factors (e.g., Ellis, 1985). Accordingly, these models tend to view resistance to change as a clinical problem that needs to be identified and ameliorated. In contrast, social constructionist models tend to view resistance as a product of the client-counselor relationship rather than as a sign of psychopathology within the client (e.g., H. Anderson, 1996; de Shazer, 1984; Watzlawick et al., 1974).

Efforts have thus been made to use resistance in the direction of change. Fisch et al. (1982), for example, have suggested that "to avoid creating . . . resistance a therapist should accept the client's statements, recognize the values [he or she] represent[s], and avoid making inflammatory or noncredible comments" (p. 101). Watzlawick et al. (1974) have suggested that resistances can even be reframed as a necessary precondition for change. Milton H. Erickson (1967), who has influenced MRI and solution-focused therapy, has described using resistance as follows:

> Any . . . possibilities constitute responsive behavior. Thus a situation is created in which the subject client can express his [or her] resistance in a constructive, cooperative fashion; manifestation of resistance by a subject is best utilized by developing a situation in which resistance serves a purpose. (p. 20)

I recall a wonderful story that Milton Erickson (1980) told that illustrates how resistance can be used to solve a problem. When Erickson was a small boy growing up on a farm, it was raining and his father was trying to bring one of their horses into the barn. His father pulled and pulled at the horse's rein, but the more he pulled the more the horse resisted and the further the horse pulled away from the barn. Little Milton observed his father's dilemma and asked if he could help. His father smiled and agreed to let Milton lend a hand. Milton sized up the situation and grabbed the horse by the rein. He then turned the horse in the opposite direction from the barn and began to pull the horse by the rein. Naturally, the horse resisted as he had for Milton's father, but this time the horse backed little Milton right into the barn. I frequently tell this story to counselors, students, and workshop attendees because it is both metaphoric and literal in its teaching of how we can use resistance in the direction of change.

Some theorists have rejected the concept of resistance altogether. De Shazer (1984) wrote a seminal article titled "The Death of Resistance," which set forth a new understanding of the phenomenon usually labeled as *resistance*. De Shazer (1982) replaced resistance with the concept of cooperating:

> Each family (individual or couple) shows a unique ways of attempting to cooperate, and the therapist's job becomes, first, to describe that particular manner to himself [or herself] that the family shows and, then, to cooperate with the family's way and, thus, to promote change. (pp. 9–10)

Along similar lines, W. H. O'Hanlon and Weiner-Davis (1989) have suggested that although "clients do not always follow therapists' suggestions . . . this is not viewed as resistance. When this happens, clients are simply educating therapists as to the most productive and fitting method of helping them change" (pp. 21–22). Indeed, the concept of cooperating represents a radical departure from the assumptions that organize traditional models insofar as it highlights the client–counselor relationship as the focal point of reciprocal, rather than unilateral, change (Guterman, 1994).

Ellis (1997b) has suggested that "viewing . . . clients' opposition[s] to change as largely 'cooperating' is interesting and cute. But it also seems to be rather naive and dishonest" (p. 61). From Ellis's viewpoint, "solution-focused counselors first teach themselves what resistant clients are 'really' like and, second, teach their clients how to helpfully change" (p. 61). I initially thought that these remarks by Ellis were reflective of his misunderstanding of my position. After thinking about it, however, I realized that, on some level, Ellis was right. When clients oppose my efforts to help them change, I still find myself at times, first, attributing such behavior to resistance. In such cases, however, I promptly remind myself that I am largely contributing to creating the resistance and, also, that I can choose to view their behavior as cooperative. Moreover, through practice I have found that I often can discern automatically my clients' responses as cooperative rather than resistive.

Whether or not we embrace the concept of resistance or cooperating (or both), the pertinent differences between theories are related to what counselors *do* in relation to their clients' oppositions. Whereas Ellis teaches REBT's theory to clients during the change process, I tend to use the client's story as the organizing metaphor during counseling. Ellis considers REBT to bring about an elegant change (i.e., disputing irrational beliefs and thereby helping clients eliminate both present and future disturbances). But I think that elegance is in the eye of the beholder. As I see it, the strategic approach in solution-focused counseling takes advantage of a window of opportunity for change that is often missed in REBT. By using the client's story, rather than the counselor's story, as the organizing metaphor during the change process, resistance can be avoided and significant change (albeit inelegant from an REBT point of view) can nevertheless be facilitated. These differences ultimately correspond to diverging ethical imperatives regarding how counselors choose to participate in the change process.

CONCLUDING REMARKS

In this chapter, postmodernism has been considered as an epistemological foundation for solution-focused counseling. Several significant clinical implications follow from a postmodern perspective and, more specifically, a social constructionist position. Clinical reality is understood as a socially constructed phenomenon, and an emphasis is placed on collaboration and enhancing cooperation. As postmodernism and social constructionism continue to evolve, these perspectives continue to clarify and enhance the theory and practice of solution-focused counseling (cf. Guterman, 1996a, 1996b).

CHAPTER 3

Problems and Change

Two fundamental and critical questions that counselors had better always ask themselves are (a) What is a problem? and (b) What is the best way to go about helping clients change? The answers to these questions serve as a guide for the selection of techniques employed in counseling. A theory of problem formation and change provides the counselor with a lens just as a pair of glasses can make clear the fuzzy world out there. Another way to think about these questions is in terms of a map that guides the counselor through the counseling process. Without a clear map, how will you know where to go? Some counselors, when asked to describe their clinical orientation, say, "I am eclectic." And this is fine if you have a clear idea in your mind of what causes problems, how to go about helping clients to change, and precisely how you will help them do that (i.e., the specific methods, interventions, and techniques that will be used). In some cases, I fear that counselors use the term *eclectic* to refer to an "anything goes" approach.

In this chapter, I describe the theory of problem formation and change that informs solution-focused counseling. This is a theory that counselors can use across cases to understand the nature of problems and change from a solution-focused perspective. I begin by describing the influences of the MRI's problem-focused model. Noteworthy is that de Shazer and his colleagues were influenced by the MRI model. In MRI, problems are conceptualized as repeated applications of ineffective solution attempts. It follows that in MRI the solution is the problem. In contrast, solution-focused therapy developed an inverse of the problem/solution ascription by proposing that the problem has within it the seeds of a solution. After a description of MRI's theory, I describe the theory of problems and change in solution-focused counseling. Then I describe solution-focused counseling's strategic approach to eclecticism. I conclude the chapter with two case examples that illustrate the model's strategic approach to eclecticism.

THE MRI'S PROBLEM-FOCUSED THEORY

In the 1950s, anthropologist Gregory Bateson (1972, 1979) was awarded a grant to study human communication and, from 1952 to 1962, headed what was referred to as "The Bateson Project." During this time, Bateson worked with Jay Haley, William Fry, and John Weakland at the Veterans Administration Hospital in California, where together they studied communication patterns of patients who had been diagnosed with schizophrenia. In 1954, Don Jackson, a psychiatrist with extensive clinical experience and a background with families, joined The Bateson Project. Bateson, Jackson, Haley, and Weakland (1956) went on to develop the famous double-bind hypothesis of schizophrenia. Jackson subsequently made pioneering contributions to the field of interactional and family therapy and in 1958 founded the MRI as a division of the Palo Alto Medical Research Foundation. The main purpose of the MRI at this time was to study schizophrenia in the context of family interactions. By the early 1960s, however, the MRI's focus expanded to include research, theory building, and training programs in a variety of areas relating to family interaction.

Rapid changes occurred at the MRI during the late 1960s. For example, Jay Haley left the MRI in 1967 to join Salvador Minuchin and Braulio Montalvo at the Philadelphia Child Guidance Clinic. Don Jackson unexpectedly died in 1968. And just prior to Jackson's death, Richard Fisch had proposed the Brief Therapy Center (BTC). Under the direction of Fisch, the BTC initially included Paul Watzlawick, Arthur Bodin, and John Weakland. The purpose of the BTC was to determine what therapeutic results could be achieved in a brief period of time (Weakland, Fisch, Watzlawick, & Bodin, 1974). Therapy was limited to 10 sessions, and an active-directive problem focus was emphasized. It was primarily in the context of the BTC that the MRI's model—the model that I hereafter refer to as *MRI*—was practiced and subsequently clarified. Influenced by the works of Bateson, Jackson, and Milton H. Erickson, MRI was developed.

Based on cybernetics, MRI holds that problems arise through the repeated application of ineffective solution attempts to ordinary life difficulties. Cybernetics is a multidisciplinary field that studies communication patterns, feedback and control, and living and mechanical systems (e.g., Maturana & Varela, 1988; Varela, 1979; von Foerster, 1984). In MRI, Watzlawick et al. (1974) have stated that *difficulties*, on one hand, refer to "an undesirable state of affairs which . . . can be resolved through some common-sense action . . . for which no special problem solving skills are necessary" (p. 38) or some "quite common life situation for which there exists no known solution and which—at least for the time being—must simply be lived with" (p. 39). *Problems*, on the other hand, refer to "impasses, deadlocks, knots, etc., which are created and maintained through the mishandling of difficulties" (Watzlawick et al., 1974, p. 39).

To illustrate MRI's theory of problem formation, Watzlawick et al. (1974) have described the commonsense approach of cheering up a depressed person.

This seems to be a logical solution. According to MRI, however, it is precisely this seemingly commonsense solution that can, in some cases, serve to exacerbate the situation. Consider, for example, the case of a wife's efforts to cheer up her depressed husband (cf. Fisch et al., 1982; Watzlawick & Coyne, 1990). Borrowing from cybernetics, the husband's depression represents a deviation from some norm. The wife might then attempt to reestablish the norm by introducing the opposite of what produced the deviance. Such efforts might take the form of the wife's attempting to cheer up her husband by encouraging him to look on the bright side. There may be instances when such a solution serves to lessen the husband's depression, and if this is so, the ensuing interaction is described as a *negative feedback loop* (Fisch et al., 1982; Watzlawick, Beavin, & Jackson, 1967; Watzlawick et al., 1974). According to cybernetics, when input from one part of the system (e.g., the husband) delivers the message that there is a deviance from some norm, any output that serves to lessen the deviation (e.g., the wife's cheering-up behavior) represents negative feedback. Watzlawick et al. (1967) have similarly stated that "in the case of negative feedback this information is used to decrease the output deviation from a set norm or bias—hence the adjective 'negative'" (p. 31).

Continuing with this example, MRI contends that introducing the opposite of depression (e.g., encouragement to look on the bright side) can also contribute to the depressed person sinking even deeper into despair. Thus it may be the case that following the wife's attempts at cheering up her husband, he becomes more depressed, which, in turn, might be followed by increased cheering-up efforts on the part of the wife (and so on). In such a case, the ensuing interaction is described as a *positive feedback loop* (Watzlawick et al., 1967, 1974). *Positive feedback* is the term used to describe cases when output (e.g., the wife's efforts to cheer up her husband) is followed by an increase or amplification of the deviation (e.g., the husband's depression). Watzlawick et al. (1967) have stated that "the same information acts as a measure for amplification of the output deviation, and is thus positive in relation to the already existing trend toward a standstill or disruption" (p. 31). Such an interaction has also been described as a *deviation-amplifying positive feedback loop*, whereby the deviation increases into a vicious interactional sequence between individuals (Fisch et al., 1982; Watzlawick et al., 1967, 1974).

The preceding discussion illustrates how attempts at solutions can contribute to an exacerbation of problems and, in effect, become the problem itself. In other words, there are countless instances in human affairs when introducing the opposite of some deviance by way of a solution attempt can actually serve to increase the deviation that the solution originally intended to lessen. Thus, when ineffective solutions are applied in a more-of-the-same manner, it can be said that the solution becomes the problem (Watzlawick et al., 1974). According to MRI, problem resolution can be facilitated by interrupting the ensuing deviation-amplifying positive feedback loops that arise when ineffective solution attempts are applied in a more-of-the-same manner. Weakland et al. (1974) have stated, for example, that "the resolution of problems . . .

primarily . . . [requires] a substitution of behavior patterns so as to interrupt the vicious, positive feedback circles" (p. 149). In conceptualizing the change process, MRI has drawn an important distinction between first-order change and second-order change (Watzlawick et al., 1974). First-order change has been defined as change "that occurs within a given system which itself remains unchanged" (Watzlawick et al., 1974, p. 146). Second-order change refers to change of change, that is, a change in the rules that govern the structure of a system or a change in the class of solutions attempted (Watzlawick et al., 1974).

Returning to the example, the more-of-the-same solution attempts on the part of the wife in response to her husband's depression can be described as a first-order change. Although the behaviors of each participant served to alter their interactions, the basic structure of the interactions remained the same (i.e., depression and cheering-up behavior occurring in a deviation-amplifying loop). A second-order change in this instance requires that the rules governing the system change thus allowing one (or each) of the participants to alter his or her class of solution attempts. The wife, for example, might surrender her efforts to cheer up her husband and, instead, agree with his bleak outlook which, in turn, could serve to reverse the cycle to a negative feedback loop (i.e., her output would be followed by a decrease in the husband's depressive behavior). The change process in MRI can frequently appear illogical and unusual. This is so, in part, because a second-order change is often applied to what, in the first-order perspective, appears to have been the solution. Watzlawick et al. (1974) have stated,

> Second-order change is introduced into the system from the outside and therefore is not something familiar or something understandable in terms of the vicissitudes of first-order change. Hence, its puzzling, seemingly capricious nature. But seen from outside the system, it merely amounts to a change of the premises . . . governing the system *as a whole*. (pp. 23–24)

MRI interventions are aimed at interrupting the problem-maintaining cycle. MRI uses numerous techniques toward this end. Ideally, MRI techniques serve to interrupt the positive feedback loops that consist of repetitive, more-of-the-same solution attempts. But for the counselor, knowing what behaviors will interrupt interactional sequences is not enough. A major focus of MRI involves maintaining therapeutic maneuverability, an integral aspect of the clinical process that directly influences the course and outcome of counseling. MRI emphasizes the importance of maintaining freedom for the counselor to work in ways that he or she thinks is best; "that is to be able to implement one's best judgment throughout the course of treatment" (Fisch et al., 1982, pp. 21–22). MRI has specified several methods for maintaining therapeutic maneuverability, including reframing, emphasizing the disadvantages of solving the problem, and encouraging clients to "go slow" in attempting to solve the problem. In particular, MRI uses reframing, a cognitive-change technique designed to enhance clients' cooperation in carrying out behavioral interventions. The intent of reframing is not to impart insight but, rather, to enable a different class of solution attempts that will interrupt some repetitive problematic sequence (Weakland et al., 1974).

SOLUTION-FOCUSED THEORY

It could be said that a clinical theory is merely a story that counselors invent to justify what they do. Something happened to Steve de Shazer and his colleagues at the Brief Family Therapy Center one evening in the 1980s that illustrates this point. That evening, while feeling stuck in a case, one of the therapists consulted with the team at the Center during a break. After getting a range of responses and suggestions from the team, someone recommended that the therapist simply ask the client to observe what happens between now and the next session that he or she wants to continue to have happen. It was felt that this would be an ideal intervention because it was positive, yet it did not ask the client to do anything new. The therapist delivered the intervention with good results. This was the beginning of what has become known as the "formula first session task" of solution-focused therapy:

> Between now and next time we meet, (we) I want you to observe so that you can tell (us) me next time, what happens in your life (or marriage or family or relationship) that you want to continue to have happen. (Molnar & de Shazer, 1987, p. 349)

This intervention was called a formula task because it did not vary in relation to whatever the presenting problem might be. It was an attempt to create a context for expecting positive things to happen. De Shazer and his colleagues, and many other solution-focused theorists, subsequently developed a growing body of knowledge in relation to this task. What follows is the theory of problems and change that informs solution-focused counseling.

Theory of Problems

The ensuing discussion of solution-focused counseling's clinical theory starts with describing the process/content distinction, a lens that I have found useful for understanding solution-focused counseling, contrasting solution-focused counseling with other clinical systems, and establishing a strategic approach to eclecticism (described later in this chapter) that is a distinctive aspect of solution-focused counseling.

Various writers have drawn a consensual distinction between the process and content aspects of counseling (e.g., Dimond, Havens, & Jones, 1978; Fraser, 1984; Guterman, 1991, 1992a, 1994, 1996a; Held, 1986, 1991, 1992, 1995; Prochaska & DiClemente, 1982). In particular, Held (1986, 1991, 1992, 1995) has recently made important contributions to this literature. According to Held, *process* refers to what clinicians do (i.e., interventions, methods, and techniques) to facilitate change. *Content* refers to the object of change in any given clinical theory. Two levels of content have also been defined by Held (1992): formal content and informal content. *Formal content* refers to the clinicians' assumptions "about what really or objectively causes . . . problems, that is, predetermined explanatory concepts that must be addressed across cases to solve problems" (p. 27). *Informal content* refers to the client's "more idiosyncratic, nonobjective assumptions about what is causing or maintaining a particular problem" (p. 27).

The clinical theory of solution-focused counseling logically follows from a social constructionist orientation. First and foremost, it is understood that we do not have access to clinical problems independent of the social interchange that occurs between counselors and clients (Guterman, 1994). Accordingly, the formal content of solution-focused counseling is defined as follows: "problems" that are cocreated in language between counselors and clients. In keeping with solution-focused theory, however, the notion of problem necessarily implies the existence of nonproblem.

> The whole concept of *problem/complaint* can be read to imply another concept, *nonproblem/noncompliant* (i.e., exceptions, times when the complaint/ problem does not happen even though the client has reason to expect it to happen) and, of course, the space between problem and nonproblem or the areas of life where the problem/nonproblem is not an issue and is not of concern to the client. This space between problem/nonproblem is also available to the client and therapist for use in constructing a solution. (de Shazer, 1991, p. 83)

In keeping with de Shazer's (1991) problem/nonproblem concept, the formal content of solution-focused counseling is thus languaging about *both* problems *and* nonproblems. Unlike those clinical models that operate consonant with modernist epistemological doctrines, solution-focused counseling's formal content does not imply what the specific "languaging about problems" might be. The formal content in psychoanalysis, for example, more specifically asserts that clinical problems comprise repressed complexes. In contrast, the formal content in solution-focused counseling is more generally stated insofar as it is contended that clinical problems are merely linguistic inventions; the specific language of such clinical problems is not specified. This difference has significant implications for how solution-focused counseling is able to organize the process and content aspects of treatment (specified further in the section on strategic eclecticism).

Another way of understanding solution-focused theory is to contrast it with MRI's theory of problem formation. In contrast to MRI, which holds that the solution attempt is the problem, solution-focused therapy holds that the problem has within it the basis of the solution. De Shazer (1991) has stated,

> Problems are seen to maintain themselves simply because they maintain themselves and because clients depict the problem as *always happening*. Therefore, times when the complaint is absent are dismissed as trivial by

Mastering the Art of Solution-Focused Counseling

the client or even remain completely hidden from the client's view. Nothing is actually hidden, but although these exceptions are open to view, they are not seen by the client as differences that make a difference. For the client, the problem is seen as primary (and the exceptions, if seen at all, are seen as secondary), while for therapists the exceptions are seen as primary; interventions are meant to help clients make a similar inversion, which will lead to the development of a solution. (p. 58)

De Shazer (1982, 1984, 1985, 1988, 1991) and his colleagues (e.g., de Shazer et al., 1986; Molnar & de Shazer, 1987; W. H. O'Hanlon & Weiner-Davis, 1989) have also commonly referred to nonproblems as exceptions. A debate has emerged regarding the usages of different terms such as *exceptions* and *unique outcomes*, the latter employed in M. White's (1988, 2000; M. White & Epston, 1990) narrative therapy. Although M. White has stated that these two terms are synonymous, de Shazer (1991) has suggested otherwise:

White (1988) states that what he calls "unique outcomes" is the same as what we call "exceptions" (de Shazer, 1985, 1988; de Shazer et al., 1986) and states that the terms are "interchangeable" (p. 8). However, the word "unique" suggests that it is a one-time event and misses the point: Exceptions are times (rather, depictions of times) when the complaint is absent; the term "exception" always has a plural form. Exceptions to the rule of the complaint are always seen as repeatable to the point where "the exception becomes the (new) rule," an idea missed entirely by the term "unique outcome" which implies nonrepeatability. (p. 83)

I see de Shazer's point. Personally, though, I use various terms to refer to what I consider to be the same phenomenon, namely, when the problem is not happening. Some of the terms I use are *exceptions, nonproblems, unique outcomes,* and *solutions.*

Theory of Change

In keeping with a social constructionist orientation, the change process in solution-focused counseling is understood as reciprocal, rather than unilateral. Thus, whereas Held (1986, 1992) has defined process as pertaining to what clinicians do to promote change—a modernist epistemological view that implies that we can unilaterally influence our clients—it is more fitting to view change processes as relating to that which counselors and clients do together. This latter conceptualization reinforces the social constructionist and postmodern position that counselors are participant–observers in language-determined systems (H. Anderson & Goolishian, 1988; Guterman, 1994). Put simply, solution-focused counseling is something that clients and counselors do together.

If process refers to the doing of counseling (i.e., interventions, methods, and techniques), then the change process in solution-focused counseling involves counselors and clients working together to identify, amplify, and increase exceptions in the direction of problem resolution. The fundamental criterion for problem resolution in solution-focused counseling is that each of the participants in the language-determined system agrees that the presenting problem is no longer a problem or is sufficiently improved. Just as the creation and maintenance of a clinical problem is contingent on social interchange, so is its resolution. In solution-focused counseling, cocreated problems "dissolve" (H. Anderson & Goolishian, 1988) when the participants in language-determined systems say they do. Often I look solely to my clients for this determination. In other instances, I find myself compelled on ethical or legal grounds to suggest otherwise. In either case, social interchange (i.e., languaging or talk) serves as the justification for problem formation and problem resolution.

However simple this theory of change may seem, I find myself challenged to articulate precisely what happens during solution-focused counseling. It is in this endeavor that the process/content distinction (and, in particular, the distinction between formal content and informal content) is integral. Clients generally enter counseling with a subjective complaint. During the problem construction stage of solution-focused counseling (detailed in chapter 5), the client and counselor work together to collaborate a problem definition that serves as the object of change. For example, the client ordinarily initiates a construction of what the problem is; the counselor might then seek clarification thereby influencing and changing the client's original problem definition (and so forth). This reciprocal and negotiating process is one in which clients and counselors both influence and are influenced by one another. Ideally, this process results in a consensual problem definition. Therefore, the coconstructed problem in solution-focused counseling takes the form of an intersubjective complaint and is understood as informal content. Informal content might take the form of "depression," "frequent arguing with a spouse," and "alcohol abuse." From my experience, however, clients and counselors usually coconstruct thicker descriptions of problems at the informal content level in solution-focused counseling. The informal content is then subsumed (for purposes of organizing the ensuing change process) by solution-focused counseling's formal content.

The main goal in solution-focused counseling is to help clients identify and amplify exceptions to the problem. There are generally two types of exceptions to a problem:

1. Something happened or did not happen that is considered a problem, such as an event or behavior (or the absence of an event or behavior), and a person coped effectively in response to the problem by doing something or resisting an impulse to do something; or
2. Something happened or did not happen that is not considered the problem.

Exceptions can be amplified by encouraging clients to do more of the behaviors that have led them to solve the problem in the past, or to observe times when they are dealing better with the problem, or ascribe significant meaning to the exceptions. In most cases, problem resolution is attributed merely to the client's own view that he or she is no longer experiencing the problem. This might be related to an increase in the client's exceptional behavior or an increase in his or her awareness of exceptions.

Strategic Eclecticism

Ginter (1988) has provoked an important dialogue regarding eclecticism in counseling circles (e.g., Blocher, 1989; Gilliland, James, & Bowman, 1994; Ginter, 1989a, 1989b; Guterman, 1991, 1992a; Hansen, 2002; Harris, 1991; Hershenson, 1992; Hershenson, Power, & Seligman, 1989a, 1989b; K. R. Kelly, 1988, 1991; Lazarus & Beutler, 1993; McBride & Martin, 1990; Nance & Meyers, 1991; Petrocelli, 2002; Simon, 1989, 1991; Weinrach, 1991). In particular, Ginter (1988) has argued that "although no single theory has all the answers, neither does the new trend toward eclecticism" (p. 6). Various counseling researchers have supported Ginter's (1988, 1989a, 1989b) suggestion that theorists and practitioners avoid developing and practicing eclectic models that combine disparate theories in an unsystematic manner.

Solution-focused counseling allows for the compatible application of diverse theories and techniques within its own clinical theory and, moreover, in a manner that enhances the facilitation of the change process. Solution-focused counseling is unique because unlike most clinical approaches, its formal content is posited in general terms, thus permitting the incorporation of virtually any informal content during the change process. The only requirement is that each of the participants in the language-determined system agrees to the chosen informal content. In effect, solution-focused counseling is a metatheory or a "process model" of counseling insofar as it is capable of reconceptualizing and reexplaining any idea (i.e., informal content) within its formal content. Another way of understanding solution-focused counseling's eclecticism is in terms of a strategic approach. The term *strategic* is used here to refer to an effort on the part of counselors to tailor conceptualizations and interventions to account for the uniqueness of each client, thereby facilitating the change process in an effective manner (and often in a brief period of time).

Solution-focused counseling also has a unique eclectic capability in cases when a client's frame of reference (informal content) is in keeping with the formal content of some other clinical approach. Thus, solution-focused counseling allows for the conceptualization of formal contents of other clinical systems as informal contents (i.e., as metaphors rather than as objective depictions of the domains of problem formation and change) that are, in turn, incorporated at solution-focused counseling's own formal content level. As an example, if a previous consumer of REBT were to attribute his or her problem to irrational beliefs (formal content), then this informal content could be used at the formal content level of solution-focused counseling during its change process (Guterman, 1994, 1996a). In solution-focused counseling, the informal content of irrational beliefs would be conceptually interpreted at the formal content of solution-focused counseling as irrational beliefs/rational beliefs. The change process would involve helping the client to identify and amplify exceptions to the problem (i.e., times when he or she is thinking and acting rationally).

The use of formal contents from other schools as informal contents within solution-focused counseling need not be restricted to instances when clients initiate such content. As participant–observers in language-determined systems, counselors not only become influenced during the change process by learning and incorporating the client's frame of reference but also teach their worldview to clients when appropriate. Thus, if appropriate for the client's problem and frame of reference, we may introduce to our clients theories from other clinical systems at the informal content level, in hopes of then using these theories at solution-focused counseling's formal content level during the change process.

The development of a strategic eclecticism for solution-focused counseling was not as easy as it appears. I struggled with these ideas and their practices for some time. When I made the shift from REBT to a solution-focused approach, I hesitated to use REBT or other modernist theories and techniques within my newfound solution-focused orientation. But something inside me still wanted to. At times I felt as if there might be utility in doing so. And then I had an insight. *If* we are all participant–observers that both influence and are influenced, *then* we as counselors cannot *not* influence our clients. So the question is not whether or not we impose our ideas on clients but, rather, how we choose to do so. If I have an idea that I think can help my client, then why not share it? Why not introduce it to my client? This stood in contrast to what I had learned in my doctoral studies, namely, always allow the client to introduce the metaphor.

Held's (1984, 1986) work in the area of strategic eclecticism also provided me with a much needed theoretical basis. Held (1986) has pointed out that process models, because they are so general with regard to articulating the content to be changed, can solve the broadest range of problems. A shortcoming of the process models, however, is that they do not tell us what content to change. The process models, like MRI and solution-focused models, tell us to look to our clients (at the informal content level) for direction. But this is sometimes not enough. Held (1986) has suggested that as proponents of process models "we seem to need content to hang our therapeutic hats on" (p. 250). There are times when our clients are seeking a more formal way of making sense of their problems. Keeney (1983) has referred to this phenomenon as "meaningful noise." Moreover, I have come to believe that in some cases there is potential utility in helping some clients understand their problems in relation to some psychological or counseling theory.

At this point, it might be helpful to draw a distinction between two types of approaches to solution-focused counseling: (a) generic and (b) eclectic. A generic approach refers to cases in which the counselor and client agree to define a problem (at the informal content level) that is void of formal content (i.e., not related to any formal theories of counseling, psychological constructs, and so forth). An eclectic approach refers to the strategic approach to eclecticism, that is, cases in which the counselor and client agree to define a problem (at the informal content level) corresponding to some formal theory of counseling, psychological construct, or other theory that might be considered formal content. In some cases, counselors will choose to adopt a generic approach. In other cases, it will be more fitting to employ a strategic approach to eclecticism.

Strategic eclecticism makes solution-focused counseling, in some cases, almost indiscernible from other clinical systems. Molnar and de Shazer (1987) have already suggested that the work of REBT's founder Albert Ellis "might . . . lead to therapeutic practices which closely resemble solution-focused tasks" (p. 351). Thus, in cases when REBT theories or techniques are used, the solution-focused counseling process might look a lot like REBT. Ellis (1977) would argue, however, that a solution-focused model that only occasionally uses REBT theories or techniques might result in "inelegant" versions of his approach. In other words, a profound philosophic change in which clients replace their core irrationalities with rational belief systems—the hallmark of Ellis's (1977) so-called elegant approach—might not be realized when using REBT within solution-focused counseling. However, a large scope of change might not be deemed necessary by the participants in the language-determined system.

In other cases, solution-focused counseling will be ostensibly similar to other clinical models. This raises the question as to what distinguishes solution-focused counseling from other models. It is noted that solution-focused counseling is distinguishable from most other clinical systems insofar as it operates consonant with a unique formal content that is capable of incorporating any informal content into its change process. Thus, unlike most clinical models, solution-focused counseling's primary emphasis is on change processes, rather than on the formal content to be changed. The following two case examples illustrate solution-focused counseling's strategic approach to eclecticism.

CASE EXAMPLES OF STRATEGIC ECLECTICISM

Codependent Some More

A 29-year-old single woman came to the first counseling session clutching Melody Beattie's (1996) best-selling book, *Codependent No More: How to Stop Controlling Others and Start Caring for Yourself.* I personally have never found codependency to be a particularly useful construct. But what shall I say to my client embracing Beattie's book so tightly? It would be unfitting in solution-focused counseling to tell my client, "I am sorry, but I don't work with codependency!"

I once attended a professional workshop held by Albert Ellis when an attendee asked his opinion about the concept of codependency. Ellis responded by stating that there is no such thing as codependency. He went on to assert that the only way that anyone could ever have an inner child—a construct used in the codependency movement—is if they were pregnant! I disagree. Although I do not favor the concept of codependency, I recognize that it is real insofar as some people believe it to be true. This is socially constructed reality. For my client and the millions of people who live by Beattie's (1996) book, codependency is not only a metaphor, but it is also a reality. If I were to challenge my client's worldview, the consequences would have been unfortunate. Moreover, accepting my client's construction of the problem and then using it in the direction of change served as a means that proved fruitful for my solution-focused ends.

In keeping with solution-focused counseling's strategic approach to eclecticism, the construct of codependency (formal content) was conceptualized as informal content. Then, the problem of codependency was conceptualized in terms of solution-focused counseling's problem/exception ascription, namely, codependency/not codependency. Counseling was organized around helping the client to define behaviorally what she considered to be codependent and then to identify and amplify exceptions to her codependent behavior. The sessions comprised various interventions, including assertiveness training and cognitive restructuring.

A Dose of Reality Therapy

I had read some of William Glasser's (e.g., 1965, 1998, 2003) work on reality therapy. So I figured that I would try my hand at including some of its principles in my own practice. Since Glasser (1965) introduced the basic principles of his model in his seminal book, *Reality Therapy: A New Approach to Psychiatry*, numerous publications have built on and embellished this simple and straightforward treatment strategy. Although a thorough discussion of reality therapy is beyond the scope of this book, I briefly describe its principles to orient readers to the following case example. According to Glasser, human beings have basic needs for love, freedom, and creativity. When people come to counseling, it is usually because they have been unable to successfully get their needs met. Furthermore, the symptoms and behaviors that are usually labeled as *psychopathology* within traditional mental health models are, instead, conceptualized as irresponsible behavior within the frame of reality therapy. The main goal in reality therapy is to help clients develop a concrete plan to work toward their goals in a responsible manner and thereby get their basic needs met.

Larry was a 32-year-old single man who was self-referred to counseling. He was employed as a clerk in a retail store. He started the first session by stating, "I am out of order." He was visibly agitated as he described the multiple problems in his life. He was in debt. He had strained relationships with his parents and siblings. He had been having conflicts with coworkers, especially his immediate supervisor. His teeth were rotting. His apartment was so cluttered that, to use his words, "It was almost condemnable." He described his life as "a total mess."

I resisted proceeding too quickly in this case given the client's multiple problems. From my experience, I have found that change often occurs more quickly when counseling proceeds slowly. Rather than jumping headstrong into the client's problems with my usual search for exceptions, I remembered the old adage, "Fools rush in." I took a deep breath and listened. And I listened. And I thought

Mastering the Art of Solution-Focused Counseling

to myself, this man needs a plan. Ah! Perhaps reality therapy might be fitting for what we are trying to do here. After all, he was not getting his needs met. His need for order. His need to have satisfactory relationships in his life.

I recalled that in the earliest phase of reality therapy it is crucial for the counselor to establish "involvement" with the client (Glasser, 1965, 1998). This is similar to what I think of as joining in solution-focused counseling. So, during much of that first session, I put most of my energy into listening and understanding and being with my client. He was clearly in emotional pain, and I sympathized with him. Toward the end of the first session, I attempted to restate the problems as he described them to me. We agreed that his life was in a shambles and that he needed a plan. In keeping with the principles of reality therapy, I asked the client to work with me to formulate a plan of action that would help him get his needs met. A plan that would help Larry get along better with his coworkers and family. A plan that would take care of his rotting teeth. A plan to work on his debt. And a plan to dig out of the mess at his apartment.

In keeping with solution-focused counseling's strategic eclecticism, the problem was conceptualized as not working on the plan/working on the plan. Counseling was organized around helping the client formulate the specifics of his plan of action and then to identify and amplify exceptions (i.e., times when he was able to effectively work on the plan). I worked with Larry over the course of the next 6 months. Our sessions involved various strategies and phases such as prioritizing goals, psychoeducation, and values clarification.

CONCLUDING REMARKS

The theory of problems and change in solution-focused counseling is offered as a map to guide counselors through the clinical process. The problem/exception conceptualization can be used across cases to understand the nature of problems and change. At the same time, the clinical theory of solution-focused counseling emphasizes the important role of the client's subjective worldview. The process/content distinction has been set forth as a lens for understanding the relationship between formal content and informal content in solution-focused counseling. In solution-focused counseling, a problem is coconstructed between the counselor and client and is understood as informal content. This informal content is then subsumed by solution-focused counseling's formal content. In addition, the strategic approach to eclecticism in solution-focused counseling allows for the compatible application of diverse theories and techniques within its clinical theory. Because the formal content of solution-focused counseling is posited in general terms, the model allows for the incorporation of virtually any content during the change process so long as each of the participants in the language system agrees to the chosen content. It follows that solution-focused counseling is to be considered a process model of counseling insofar as it is capable of reconceptualizing any informal content within its formal content.

CHAPTER 4
Before the First Session

We usually think the start of counseling to be when the client comes to the first session. If we look at what happens outside of counseling sessions and think in terms of noncounseling events as the source of much, if not all, change that occurs, then one of the most fruitful times for change seems to be *before* the first session. It is before the first session that clients make the momentous decision to seek help. This decision is usually made due to various factors. The problem might have gotten so out of hand that the client feels he or she cannot handle it anymore. Perhaps a loved one has recommended he or she seek professional help. In some instances, a person might be mandated to counseling by a law enforcement agency or an employer. Regardless of the reason, when someone picks up the telephone and requests a counseling appointment, this is usually a time like no other and the person is ready for change.

Most counselors already intervene with their clients, on some level, before the first session in order to get things rolling. Depending on how the practice is set up, the counselor or an office worker usually makes a telephone contact with the client and conducts a brief telephonic intake to determine the presenting problem, and then he or she will exchange telephone numbers and addresses, provide directions to the office, set the first appointment, discuss fees, collect insurance information, and so forth. But so much more can be done at this critical stage. For example, the counselor can begin to define goals with the client. The counselor might also ask the client to begin identifying exceptions to the problem. As a result, the counselor might create an expectancy for change that can, in turn, be amplified in ensuing counseling sessions.

This chapter is about tapping the inevitability of change that occurs prior to the first counseling session. It is about striking while the iron is hot. By recognizing that change occurs before the first session and then doing something proactive to help facilitate this phenomenon, counselors can help clients bring about problem resolution and change in a quicker and more effective manner. In this chapter, I offer several strategies to bring about change before the first session.

AN ACCIDENTAL DISCOVERY

In recent years, a growing literature has addressed *pretreatment change*, a phenomenon that has been identified within the context of solution-focused clinical models as a basis from which to quickly resolve problems (Allgood, Parham, Salts, & Smith, 1995; Guterman, 1998; Lawson, 1994; Ness & Murphy, 2002; Throckmorton, Best, & Alison, 2001; Weiner-Davis, de Shazer, & Gingerich, 1987). Remember that one of the main goals in solution-focused counseling is to help clients identify and build on exceptions to their problems. Exceptions are defined as times when the problem does not happen even though the client has reason to expect it to happen. Weiner-Davis et al. (1987) provided the first account of their "accidental discovery" in which it was found that some clients reported during the first session that positive changes (i.e., exceptions) had occurred in relation to their presenting problem between the time they called for the initial appointment and the time they came in for the first session; hence, pretreatment change. It was hypothesized by Weiner-Davis et al. that by identifying pretreatment change during the first session, problem resolution and goal attainment could be achieved in a quicker manner than if such change were not identified. Weiner-Davis et al. conducted a survey aimed at assessing the extent to which clinicians can help clients to identify pretreatment change during the first session. In their survey of 30 clients, they found that in 20 cases (66.6%) pretreatment change was reported. In a replication of this study, Lawson (1994) found that in 82 cases, 49 clients (59.7%) reported pretreatment change. Lawson set forth the following script for counselors to use during the first session:

> Our center is conducting a research project and the researchers are curious about a particular issue. It seems that many times people notice in between the time they make an appointment for counseling and the first session, that some things seem different.
>
> 1. Have you noticed changes with your problem situation since our telephone conversation?
> 2. (If yes to #1): Do these changes relate to the reason you came for counseling?
> 3. (If yes to #1): Are these the kinds of changes you would like to continue to have happen? (p. 245)

Lawson (1994) provided the following case example to illustrate the identification of pretreatment change during the first session:

> A single mother with three children came for counseling because her 15-year-old son, to use her words, "made a complete turn around in his behavior" over a 3-month period. His grades had dropped from As and Bs

to Ds and Fs, and he was going to fail the ninth grade if a drastic change did not take place in his study habits and commitment to school. He was also skipping school, sneaking out of the house at night after everyone had gone to bed, and lying about his nightly excursions. The mother and son had . . . numerous meetings with school personnel, including the teacher, principal, and counselor, but with no significant results. When she made the initial contact for counseling, she stated that she was so frustrated with her son's behavior that she was seeking possible residential settings for her son if counseling was not successful. In her own words she had ". . . tried everything and nothing has worked." On questioning her about the differences in the problem since she made the initial appointment 2 weeks before, she noted that her son's behavior had begun to change for the better, but that she was suspicious about the sincerity of the change. She was not sure exactly what brought about the change but did consider the change as the type of changes she wanted to see continue.

With further questioning about what she was doing differently about her son's behavior over the last 2 weeks, she stated that she thought her son knew she was very serious about sending him off to a residential setting if his behavior did not improve. The son confirmed the mother's explanation. From that point, the sessions revolved around making a distinction between times when the son knew she was serious about her expectations and when she exhibited less resolve about her expectations for his behavior. Specific behaviors were then discussed. Once the mother's solution behaviors were clarified, focus was placed on how the mother could maintain consistency in implementing them. With the solution behaviors identified, sessions revolved around refining and building on what was working (e.g., addressing logical and natural consequences, discussing ways the son could earn back trust and subsequently more freedom, involving the mother and son in enjoyable activities together). (p. 246)

IDENTIFYING PRETREATMENT CHANGE *BEFORE* THE FIRST SESSION

While working for a managed care company in the 1990s, I considered how to build on the studies that had already been conducted in the area of pretreatment change. It occurred to me that a next step could be to formulate an intervention in which a telephone contact is made with clients *before* the first session. I hypothesized that doing so might serve to increase the frequency of the identification of pretreatment change during the initial counseling session as compared to the incidences of pretreatment change found in previous studies (Lawson, 1994; Weiner-Davis et al., 1987).

But just when I thought I had come across a novel variation of the study of pretreatment change, I learned that Duncan, Miller, and Sparks (2004), S. D. Miller (1992), and Talmon (1990) had already applied this approach in their clinical work. Miller has stated that he "now requests that all clients observe for the presence of . . . [pretreatment change] between the scheduling of and attendance at the first appointment" (1992, p. 9). There nevertheless remained a lack of literature that explicated interventions aimed at identifying pretreatment change before the first session. Accordingly, I decided to implement a preintake telephone contact in my work (Guterman, 1998).

Once an intake appointment was established, I attempted to make a telephone contact with the client. During the telephone conversation, I confirmed the appointment date, time, and location; briefly discussed the presenting problem; and then delivered the following solution-focused task:

> Often people find that in between the time when they make an appointment for counseling and the first session, there have been times when they have dealt better with the problem. I have found that identifying these times during our first session can help us work toward a solution to the problem. So between now and our first appointment, I would like you to observe so that you can tell me during our first session about those times when you found that you were dealing better with the problem. This might include times when you coped better, solved the difficulty, or experienced even a small change in a positive direction.

At some point during the first session, I reminded the client of the telephone contact and asked a follow-up question aimed at helping the client identify exceptions to the presenting problem. The follow-up question was stated as follows: "Tell me about those times when you found that you were dealing better with the problem." If the client was able to identify exceptions, then this was considered to be an incidence of pretreatment change. If the client stated that there were no exceptions, then I asked about small changes. This question was stated as follows: "Tell me about those times when you found that you were dealing better with the problem even in a small way." (As mentioned in chapter 1, a small change often leads to big results. As I show in the next chapter, if clients are unable to identify exceptions, counselors can ask them to consider small signs of improvement. Doing so often uncovers exceptions that can be amplified in the direction of change.) If the client was able to identify small changes prior to the first session, then this was considered to be an incidence of pretreatment change. If the client was unable to identify small changes, then it was considered that pretreatment change did not occur. In keeping with social constructionist thinking, the criterion for determining whether or not pretreatment change occurred was that both the counselor and the client reached a consensual agreement that exceptions had occurred since the telephone contact (i.e., there were times when the client was dealing better with the presenting problem). Following is a case example.

> A 39-year-old married male told me during the pre-intake telephone conversation that he had a "sex problem." The client specified that his wife

had urged him to seek help because of his frequent masturbating. The client stated that he masturbated on at least a daily basis and as a result usually had little desire to have sex with his wife. During the telephone conversation, I inquired about times when he was able to resist masturbating on any given day. The client reported that on the rare occasions when he did not masturbate he would usually have sex with his wife. I suggested that the client attempt to repeat this solution and be prepared to discuss in the first session how he had been able to resist masturbating.

The client came to the first session accompanied by his wife. The client reported that he had resisted masturbating on 3 days since the telephone contact, that he had sex with his wife on 2 of these days, and that he had done this by reminding himself of how pleased his wife had been in the past when he had satisfied her sexually. The client's wife confirmed this report and jokingly expressed concern that further progress would be "too much" for her. It was agreed that pretreatment change had occurred. At the end of the second session, the husband, the wife, and I agreed that the sex problem was resolved and other treatment goals were identified, including improving communication between the couple.

Making a preintake telephone contact in this case afforded me with an opportunity to make an assessment and implement an intervention before the first session, including a clear definition of the problem and treatment goal, and identification of exceptions. Doing so also contributed to establishing a focused treatment approach during the intake and in subsequent sessions. It follows that although initial telephonic contacts should not take the place of in person assessments, the telephone can be used to make the intake process more efficient and effective. (Guterman, 1998, pp. 372–373)

In my survey of 74 clients, 58 reported pretreatment change (78.3%). This supported my hypothesis that a preintake telephone call would serve to increase the frequency of the identification of pretreatment change during the initial counseling session as compared with the incidences of pretreatment change found in the previous studies by Weiner-Davis et al. (1987) and Lawson (1994). One might argue that a potential limitation of the studies conducted by Weiner-Davis et al. (1987), Lawson (1994), and myself (Guterman, 1998) lies in the role that counselors play in influencing clients to identify pretreatment change. Lawson (1994) has suggested that "perhaps respondents would have reported fewer pretreatment changes if survey questions had been worded in a more neutral fashion" (p. 247). Lawson (1994) has also suggested, however, that the bias inherent in the methodology used in the pretreatment change studies be considered as a strength rather than a weakness. According to Lawson, "the purposive nature of the survey questions . . . was based on the view that counselors and clients cocreate problem and solution realities and that cocreated solutions produce durable change" (p. 247).

If we accept the social constructionist position from which solution-focused counseling is informed, namely, that counselors are participant–observers in language-determined systems and hence we cannot be neutral, then it is also important to recognize the necessary connection between the researcher and the observed. Rather than restrict our attention to traditional quantitative methodologies designed to attain objective knowledge, an alternative research paradigm is needed for pretreatment change inquiry. Given the reciprocal influences of counselors and clients during change processes in solution-focused counseling, it seems only fitting that the research methods used in this area would be collaborative and therefore in keeping with qualitative methods of inquiry. In qualitative methods, it is understood that the researcher is the primary instrument for data collection and data analysis.

Nevertheless, research continues along quantitative lines in the area of pretreatment change. Such research has studied different variables regarding the phenomenon of pretreatment change, including the relationship between the incidence of pretreatment change and outcome effectiveness, the degree to which making a preintake telephone contact reduces the frequency of clients not showing for their first appointments, and assessing the effects that making a preintake telephone contact and identifying pretreatment change has on the number of counseling sessions needed to resolve the presenting problem.

DELIVERING INTERVENTIONS *BEFORE* THE FIRST SESSION

Toward the end of the 1990s, my thinking about pretreatment change began to change. It occurred to me that pretreatment change was not a phenomenon "out there" to be discovered by counselors. Instead, it was a phenomena that was cocreated between the client and the counselor. If pushed to the logical extreme, it follows that an effective solution-focused counselor might realize 100% success at identifying pretreatment change. This led me to rethink my role and function in relation to pretreatment change strategies. Pretreatment change is not to be considered as a research endeavor but, rather, as an intervention. It is something that counselors do with clients—like other interventions, tasks, or procedures—designed to achieve a therapeutic goal or outcome.

In recent years, I have also found the prevailing pretreatment interventions to be a bit Pollyannaish. When I conducted my pretreatment study, I called my clients on the telephone before they came in for the first session and, without knowing much about the problem or ever having met the client, asked them to observe for times when they found that they were dealing better with the problem. I suspect that probably half or more of these clients listened with a deaf ear to my request (Guterman, 1998). I now call my clients before the first session not for purposes of a study, but for the end of counseling itself. My purpose is to make a brief contact with the client and create a cooperative context for the forthcoming counseling process. One of the byproducts of calling my clients before the first session is that it has reduced the number of no shows and cancellations. Once my office is notified of a new referral, I routinely call the client and introduce myself. Our conversation usually lasts about

5 minutes, but can sometimes go longer. I start by saying that I like to call my clients to get a sense of what has brought them to seek counseling, what they are expecting, and that sort of thing. I tell them that this information is helpful to me as I try to be of assistance to them, and I also tell them that many of my clients have told me that doing so has been of help to them.

I might start by inquiring about the presenting problem. Once the client begins to describe the problem, I might or might not seek clarification. This contact also gives me a chance to assess what, if any, causes the client might attribute to his or her problem. This, in turn, serves as useful information during counseling when considering whether I will follow a generic or an eclectic approach. In some cases, with the client's permission, a family member will also get on the telephone and provide input. In such cases, my preference is for the family member to get on another telephone extension and speak with me while the client is still on the telephone. In some cases, I choose to inquire about exceptions. In other cases, I do not. I might, for example, ask the client, "When has there been a time when you have noticed that you coped better with this problem?" Or, instead, I might ask the client to observe for times when he or she is coping better with the problem.

I have experimented with many different approaches to making contact with clients before the first session. At the very least, doing so provides an opportunity to join with the client and establish a cooperative working relationship. Such contact can also establish a starting point for the early stages of solution-focused counseling, including coconstructing a problem and identifying and amplifying exceptions. With the proliferation of the Internet, an increasing number of counselors will be using this medium and other forms of technology to enhance the pretreatment change process and counseling in general (Guterman & Kirk, 1999). For example, rather than calling clients on the telephone, clients might be directed to a Web site or be sent instructions via e-mail regarding solution-focused principles. Following is a case example that illustrates the use of solution-focused techniques before the first session.

A MAN IN SEARCH OF HIS OLD SELF

Myers and Harper (2004) have noted that although persons over the age of 60 make up approximately 13% of the total United States population, they account for only 6% to 8% of persons seen in mental health settings. Some researchers have suggested that barriers to the use of mental health services by this population might include bias toward older persons among service providers, including counselors (Myers & Harper, 2004; Nordhus & VandenBos, 1998). These biases can take many forms. For example, some counselors might think that older persons, because of their advanced age, are simply not amenable to or interested in counseling. Myers and Harper (2004) have suggested, however, that "the fact that older persons respond to interventions as well as or better than persons who are younger suggests the need for counselors to address issues of age bias in order to help overcome the current lack of service to this population" (p. 215). The following case illustrates the use of solution-focused techniques before the first session and, also, the counselor's receptiveness to working with an older client.

A 73-year-old White married man named Seymour was referred to counseling by his primary care physician. The counselor called the client the day after the initial appointment was made. In their telephone conversation, Seymour was friendly and verbose. He stated that he had been diagnosed with major depressive disorder 2 years ago following a myocardial infarction. He stated that he experienced limited improvement after trying several antidepressants. The client stated that since becoming depressed he seldom engaged in recreational or social activities and was anhedonic (i.e., unable to experience pleasure in normally pleasurable acts). After talking to Seymour about his problem for several minutes, the counselor asked him, "What is your goal in counseling?" Seymour stated that his goal was to become his "old self" again.

The counselor considered that the client's depression was, to some degree, endogenous insofar as it related to the myocardial infarction. But the counselor also considered that he might be amenable to solution-focused counseling. The counselor asked the client to describe, in behavioral terms, what being his old self was like. He stated that when he was his old self, he was very active, socialized frequently, and enjoyed activities of daily living. The counselor then asked Seymour to think of any time in the past week when he found that he was being his old self. Seymour recalled that there were one or two times when he was being more active or had socialized. He maintained, however, that these exceptions were not significant. At the end of the telephone conversation, the counselor asked the client to observe times when he found he was able to be his old self again, even in a small way.

Seymour arrived at the first session accompanied by his wife. At the start of the first session, the client smiled and stated, "I am my old self again!" Seymour's wife confirmed that her husband had made significant progress during the past week. The counselor proceeded to ask the client and his wife to identify the many instances in the past week when he was being his old self. Various exceptions to depression were identified, including the client's initiating a card game one evening with a couple that he and his wife had previously socialized with on a regular basis. During the second session, held 1 week later, the client was encouraged to continue to do more of the exceptions. At the third session, held 2 weeks later, the client and his wife reported continued progress. During the fourth session, it was agreed that the client was being his old self again and that further sessions were not needed at this time. It was agreed that the client could resume counseling in the future if he felt himself slipping away from being his old self. Three months later, the counselor made a telephonic follow-up. The client reported that he was still being his old self and that he was feeling much less depressed. The client was again advised that he may resume counseling if he ever felt the need. The counselor never heard from Seymour again.

In this case, the preintake telephone contact provided the counselor with an opportunity to assess the client's goals and expectations of counseling. The

Mastering the Art of Solution-Focused Counseling

client set the goal of becoming his old self during the preintake telephone contact and thereby established a foundation for solution-focused conceptualization and intervention.

CONCLUDING REMARKS

An increasing literature has reported research on the phenomenon of *pretreatment change*. In solution-focused counseling, making a preintake telephone contact can afford counselors with an opportunity to join with the client, make an initial assessment, and implement an intervention before the first session. Doing so can also contribute to establishing a focused treatment approach during the intake and subsequent sessions. Although initial telephonic contacts should not take the place of in-person assessments, the telephone can be used to make the intake process more efficient and effective.

CHAPTER 5
The First Session

In this chapter, I describe the process followed during the first session in solution-focused counseling. The following explication is meant to serve as a guide that will inevitably require detours. Because each client is unique, the explication does not account for the nuances that are distinctive to each case. The process is meant to be used during the initial session. Nevertheless, the recursive (i.e., interrelated, overlapping, and circular) nature of the solution-focused counseling process makes it applicable to subsequent sessions. Despite its recursive aspects, the process is explicated in terms of discrete stages. These stages, however, are not meant to be understood as having clear and impermeable boundaries. The stages during the first session consist of (a) joining with the client, (b) coconstructing a problem and goal, (c) identifying and amplifying exceptions, and (d) coconstructing tasks.

JOINING WITH THE CLIENT

At the start of every counseling session, especially the first session, I begin by greeting my client. I make every effort to show an interest in my client, make eye contact, and respect his or her views and opinions. These are fundamental counseling skills, but I consider them integral to the solution-focused approach because of the model's collaborative, rather than educative, approach. Joining with the client is not to be understood as a discrete phase of counseling but, rather, as something that is done throughout the treatment process. I have chosen to identify this aspect of counseling under a separate heading, however, to underscore the importance of making a connection with the client during the earliest stage of counseling.

The contexts in which I have worked have had different policies regarding whether or not a formal intake is to be conducted during the first session. Some settings have required that I conduct a comprehensive intake, including a psychosocial history, mental status examination, and multiaxial diagnostic impression in keeping with the *DSM*. Other settings have not required any of these elements. Others have fallen somewhere in between. Regardless of where I am working, I find that I am always constrained by my context to some degree. If I am working in a setting that requires comprehensive assessments, then I run the risk of doing too little. If I work in a setting that does not favor doing formal assessments and I do a thorough mental status examination, then I might be accused of being too pathologizing.

My preference is to conduct a formal intake. So I usually begin the solution-focused counseling process by obtaining a psychosocial history, conducting a mental status examination, and formulating a multiaxial diagnostic impression. Conducting a mental status examination allows me to assess suicide and homicide risk, psychotic thinking, and clinical depression, and thereby maintain standard practices in the mental health profession. The intake also provides an opportunity to discuss with the client various legal and ethical issues in keeping with the *ACA Code of Ethics* (ACA, 2005), including limits of confidentiality, the counseling relationship, and professional responsibility. I also find that conducting a formal psychosocial history can serve to identify exceptions that might otherwise not have been revealed had an intake not been conducted. When inquiring about a client's interests, hobbies, and social life, exceptions to the problem are often uncovered. For example, one client told me during the first session of her numerous recreational activities and her extensive social network. In addition, her history revealed that she had several chronic physical illnesses that were related to her reason for seeking counseling. As I proceeded through the psychosocial history, a number of exceptions came out with regard to her ability to cope with her physical problems.

The history-taking process is often aided by telling clients at the outset, "I would like to start by taking a few minutes to obtain some background information." Phrasing it in this way often speeds up what would otherwise be a time-consuming process of collecting background information. My clients usually appreciate my thoroughness, and in addition, the intake gives me an opportunity to join with my clients and establish a cooperative relationship. Again, although joining with clients is an ongoing process in counseling, it is particularly crucial at this early stage. After completing the formal assessment phase of the session, I shift to the next stage, coconstructing a problem and goal.

COCONSTRUCTING A PROBLEM AND GOAL

When I first started in the field, I was frequently warned by professors and supervisors, "Don't create a problem!" This made a lot of sense to me because I was operating from a worldview that held that there are real problems "out there" and my job was to help the client identify those real problems, not imaginary ones that I might unwittingly foist upon them. I still share this caveat— Don't create a problem!—to the extent that I think we had better be mindful of not imposing pathological or other unhelpful problem definitions on clients. For

Mastering the Art of Solution-Focused Counseling

me, this is one of my principal ethical imperatives. However, in the postmodern world there are no problems per se but, rather, problems are coconstructed. If we accept the social constructionist view that "real" is only what a group of people have decided to call real, then a problem in counseling becomes real only when a counselor and a client join together and define it as such. Thus, the proper question is, How shall we go about cocreating a solvable problem for counseling? As Jay Haley (1976) has suggested, "If therapy is to end properly, it must begin properly by negotiating a solvable problem" (p. 9).

The process of coconstructing a problem may be started by simply asking the client, "What is the problem that brings you here today?" There are many variations to this question. The notion of a problem can be bypassed altogether by asking the client, "What brings you here today?" Counselors can also frame the question in goal-setting terms by asking, "What would you like to accomplish through counseling?" Regardless of the questioning used, it is important during this stage to coconstruct a goal along with the problem. When developing goals, it is preferable to do so in positive (rather than negative) language (i.e., as an increase of something, rather than as a decrease of something). As Walter and Peller (1993) have noted, "it is impossible to make a picture of something not happening" (p. 80). In the case of anger, for example, the goal of decreasing anger does not allow for a vivid picture of the desired outcome. In contrast, the goal of increasing effective coping skills for anger is stated in positive terms.

In many cases, counselors can help clients to specify the problem by requesting that they provide a video description of the problem (W. H. O'Hanlon & Weiner-Davis, 1989). A video description is a verbal account that provides an accurate mental image of an event. To obtain a video description, a client might be asked, "If 100 people saw the problem happening, and furthermore, if they all agreed that the same thing was happening, what would it be that they would all agree had happened?" All too often, vague problem definitions (e.g., unhappiness) and vague goals (e.g., finding oneself) result in an endless course of treatment. Of course, there are always exceptions. In some cases, it might be preferable to generalize the problem and the goal due to its rigid specificity. Following is a case example.

A married couple presented to counseling, and the wife's presenting complaint was that her husband always kicks his shoes off in the hallway when he arrives home from work. I saw that this problem definition might limit the possibilities for identifying exceptions. The wife and I then agreed to construct a goal in more general terms which, in turn, allowed for more possibilities. The wife was encouraged to define the goal as, "My husband will be more helpful with the housework." The husband agreed with this goal, and the treatment process was then organized around identifying exceptions (e.g., times when either the wife or the husband observed that the husband was helpful with the housework). Coconstructing a relevant problem and a solvable goal is often an arduous process. Sometimes attempts at working through the solution-focused counseling stages will fail precisely because an attainable goal was not developed. For example, in the case just described, a successful outcome might have been impeded if the husband refused to cooperate. In such instances, it is important for counselors to determine who the "customer" is and construct goals accordingly.

In some cases, the problem or the goal might be too large in scope. Bipolar disorder, for example, is a large problem definition. Some counselors and clients might even argue that bipolar disorder is an unsolvable problem. For those clients with chronic mental illness who are also noncompliant with their prescribed medications, initially helping them be compliant with their medication regimen is often an attainable and relevant goal. Limiting the scope of the goal can also serve to instill hope for many clients, especially for those who complain that they have failed in prior treatment.

Construction of a problem and a goal that fits with the client's idiosyncratic frame of reference is perhaps most important. In a case involving a divorced woman, for example, the client defined the problem as loneliness (Guterman, 1996a). I assumed that the goal would be to eliminate loneliness. The client, however, helped me understand that her goal was to cope with, rather than eliminate, loneliness. The client understood loneliness as a given in her life on the basis of her inability thus far to find a suitable mate. The client was also unwilling to settle for an unhealthy relationship, a strength (and, hence, an exception) that I promptly identified and amplified. We eventually reached a consensus that the goal of counseling would be to increase her effective coping skills for loneliness.

In another case, a man described himself as a problem drinker. During the initial session, I learned that the client had resisted previous mental health professionals who claimed that he was an "alcoholic" and that he should abstain from alcohol entirely. The client held that he was capable of reducing his alcohol intake. Rather than re-creating the resistance that led the client to drop out of treatment in the past, I viewed the client's position as useful information rather than as resistance. A cooperative counseling relationship was maintained by accepting the client's position and working with it.

When coconstructing problems and goals, I look to the client for guidance in selecting a fitting metaphor (i.e., informal content). In keeping with a social constructionist orientation, I resist being lured into a search for the "correct" problem—unless, of course, my clients have bought into such a search. Instead, I justify my coconstructions in terms of a fit with the clients' worldview. In the case of the problem drinker, my participation was informed by the social constructionist position that I do not hold an objective (i.e., independent of the observer) view of what is (and is not) a problem. Instead, the problem and the goal were constructed in a collaborative manner between the client and myself.

A Generic or an Eclectic Approach?

It is crucial to learn how the client makes sense of the problem (i.e., what, if any, cause the client might attribute to the problem). In particular, it is important to assess whether the client attributes the problem to a formal theory, such as a psychological construct, school of thought, or paradigm. In a case described in chapter 3, for example, the client attributed her problem to codependency. In keeping with solution-focused counseling's clinical theory, the problem was conceptualized as codependency/not codependency. The problem construction stage involved obtaining a description of what the client does when she is thinking, feeling, and acting codependently. Exceptions were then identified and amplified in the direction of change.

If the client does not attribute the problem to some other clinical theory or if you, the counselor, assess that it is not useful to introduce another clinical theory, then follow what I have previously referred to as a generic approach to solution-focused counseling. By generic, I mean that the client's idiosyncratic worldview serves as the principal method for the selection of the informal content to be used during the stage of coconstructing the problem. However, if the client attributes the problem to some other clinical theory or if you, the counselor, assess that some clinical theory is a useful metaphor and choose to introduce it to the client, then follow the eclectic approach to solution-focused counseling. Sometimes it will be clear that a client embraces the formal content corresponding to another theory, and thus this might serve as a useful metaphor to use in solution-focused counseling. In other cases, a client might discover some theory after having had several sessions of solution-focused counseling. For example, the client might have found a self-help book or spoken to a friend about a particular model in between sessions.

In some cases, you might choose to introduce to the client the formal content from another model. In such instances, it is crucial to assess whether the formal content from the other model fits with the client's worldview. Will the client accept the theory? Does the theory fit with the client's understanding of the problem? If not, presenting the theory might create resistance and impede the change process and therefore run counter to the goals of solution-focused counseling. If an eclectic approach is followed, then it might be necessary to institute an educative phase in which the client is taught the principles of the model and its associated techniques. Consider the following case.

Case Example

A 29-year-old woman presented with the goal of changing her husband (e.g., increasing his willingness to spend more time with her, increasing the times when he invites her to participate in his hobbies). Unfortunately, the husband refused to come to any of the sessions. According to the wife, the husband stated that she was the one who needed to change. I suggested to the client that the only one she could change was herself, but I also proposed that the changes she would make might also serve to influence her husband in positive ways. The client, however, seemed to lack any notion of how she might do this. Furthermore, attempts at identifying exceptions (e.g., times when the wife had been able to favorably influence her husband) were unsuccessful. Accordingly, the second session involved an educative phase that included teaching the client (a) how to use cognitive techniques to cope with her anger and (b) how to provide immediate positive reinforcement of those behaviors by her husband that she deemed favorable. The wife reported during the third session that she was feeling less angry toward her husband and that she had begun rewarding him for any signs of desired behavior. Correspondingly, she observed that her husband was kind to her on a more frequent basis.

This case illustrates some important aspects of solution-focused counseling. For example, it demonstrates that the stage of coconstructing a problem and a goal sometimes takes several sessions and that in some cases it is preferable to refrain from proceeding to subsequent stages during the initial session. This case also exemplifies solution-focused counseling's strategic approach to eclecticism. It was consensually agreed by the wife and counselor that the goal was to apply cognitive and behavioral techniques aimed at influencing the husband in favorable ways. The cognitive and behavioral principles served as informal content that was, in turn, subsumed within solution-focused counseling's formal content. The change process involved the wife's application of cognitive and behavioral techniques and the identification and amplification of exceptions (i.e., times when the wife found that she was effective at using these techniques to influence her husband).

IDENTIFYING AND AMPLIFYING EXCEPTIONS

Identifying Exceptions

From my experience, there are always exceptions to clients' problems. Addicts resist using drugs, depressives have up days, and oppositional adolescents comply with the rules. The problem is that sometimes clients do not recognize these exceptions. By helping clients identify and examine these exceptions, we can help them work toward solutions.

The first rule of thumb when asking questions aimed at identifying and amplifying exceptions is to watch your language. In particular, presuppositional questioning refers to using questions as interventions (W. H. O'Hanlon & Weiner-Davis, 1989). For example, it is important to ask, "*When* has there been a time when you coped better with the depression?" rather than, "*Has there* been a time when you coped better with the depression?" The latter is a yes-or-no question that leaves room for the client to respond negatively. The former carries with it a sense of expectancy that there indeed have been times when the client has coped better with depression. Often there is a silent response from clients, because many (if not most) clients are not accustomed to being asked at such an early stage in treatment about times when things are going better. This questioning is interventive insofar as it produces a sudden shift in the client's problem focus. The counselor should be comfortable with the silence and give the client time to digest this line of questioning.

If the client identifies exceptions, then proceed to amplify these (see the next section). If, however, the client states that there have been no exceptions, then encourage the client to consider small differences. Clients can frequently recall exceptions when asked to consider small changes that have occurred. It has also been found that small changes often lead to bigger changes. If the client is unable to identify small differences, then identify *potential exceptions.*

Sometimes counselors become frustrated when clients are unable, are unwilling, or otherwise do not identify exceptions. In such cases, it is suggested that counselors do not view this occurrence as resistance, but as useful information. The client might be so problem-focused that it is necessary for the counselor to help him or her visualize what a solution would look like. Questions aimed at identifying potential exceptions might take the form of asking, "What will it be like when you are coping better with the problem?" This process is derived from de Shazer's (1978) Crystal Ball Technique, which involves encouraging clients to picture themselves in a future situation in which they are functioning satisfactorily. Molnar and de Shazer (1987) have noted that "the 'Crystal Ball Technique' came to be regarded as a precursor of a solution focus, in that it was an early attempt to systematically focus the client on solutions rather than on problems" (p. 350).

Similar to the Crystal Ball Technique is the miracle question, one of the most widely practiced solution-focused techniques:

> Suppose that one night there is a miracle and while you are sleeping the problem that brought you into therapy is solved: How would you know? What would be different? (de Shazer, 1988, p. 5)

The miracle question can serve to identify potential exceptions in cases when the client was previously unable to do so. Imagining that the problem is solved can help the client consider precisely what will be different when the goal is reached. Hence, this question can go a long way in helping to identify potential exceptions. Moreover, once clients entertain the miracle, they are sometimes able to identify real life exceptions.

At this point, let me share some caveats about the miracle question (cf. Shilts, Rambo, & Huntley, 2003). Sometimes, this question is asked by counselors, especially new counselors, in a rigid, abrupt, and formal manner. Sometimes it is asked too early in treatment when the client is so problem-focused that he or she is not ready for such a line of questioning. It is important to consider that in counseling, like so many other things in life, timing is everything. And there are so many different ways to ask the miracle question so that it fits with the client's way of making sense of the problem. I prefer to ask the question in more realistic terms. So I might ask the client, "How would things be if they were going a little better? What would be different?" Despite your efforts, in some cases, clients are unable to identify exceptions or potential exceptions. When this happens, it is helpful to consider either clarifying the problem or cocreating a task designed to identify potential exceptions or a goal (see the section on coconstructing tasks).

Amplifying Questions

If exceptions are identified, the client is helped (through various lines of questioning) to amplify and ascribe meaning to these exceptions. One of the main functions of amplifying exceptions is to help clients identify the differences between the times when they have the problem and the times when they do not. An example of such questioning might be, "How did you make that happen?" W. H. O'Hanlon & Weiner-Davis (1989) have stated that "verbalizing . . . [differences] produces clarity both for us and for our clients. Once our clients identify how they get good things to happen, they will know what it will take to continue in this vein" (p. 86). Another purpose of the amplification process is to empower clients with a sense of self-efficacy (Bandura, 1997). Following is a list of the amplifying questions that I most frequently use in solution-focused counseling.

- *How did you make that happen?* This question is designed to identify specific behaviors that led to the change that was recognized as an exception. This question is also aimed at creating a context for establishing a sense of self-efficacy for the client, which is also brought about by the other amplifying questions listed here.
- *How did it make your day go differently?* This question is designed to make a connection between exceptions and good things happening in other areas of the client's life. This speaks to the snowball effect that exceptions can have in clients' lives and the principle that a small change can lead to big results. We have all heard of kicking the dog when we are upset or angry about something else, but sometimes when good things happens (i.e., exceptions), this spills over in positive ways in other areas of our lives, too.
- *Who else noticed?* This is a useful question if there are other people in counseling sessions such as family members. But this question can also be posed if no one else is present in the session. This question helps identify differences that the client might have otherwise not considered.
- *How is that different from how you have dealt with the problem in the past?* This question helps clients recognize differences between new behaviors and past problem-solving behaviors that were not effective.
- *What did you tell yourself to make it happen?* This question is a throwback from my early training and experience in REBT and cognitive therapy. Without necessarily going into great detail about the theory of REBT or cognitive therapy, I offer this question to clients in an effort to help them identify the coping self-statements that might correspond to their exceptions.
- *What does this say about you and your ability to deal with this problem?* This question is aimed at eliciting a response to the effect, "I guess I am capable of solving this problem." I adapted this question from Michael White's narrative therapy approach (M. White, 2000; M. White & Epston, 1990) in which clients are helped to ascribe new meaning to the unique outcomes in their lives and thereby construct new stories, a process he calls restorying.

- *What are the possibilities?* Similar to the preceding question, this question is aimed at ascribing a sense of hope, optimism, and determination in relation to the problem and goal. This question was also adapted from M. White's narrative therapy model.

Encouraging clients to provide thick descriptions (Geertz, 1973) of the changes that occasion their exceptions can be particularly helpful in creating new meaning. Using the just listed questions in a variety of creative ways can assist in this process. It is also important for counselors to be aware of the tendency for clients to offer thin descriptions of their positive changes. For example, it is not uncommon for clients to account for their progress with sayings such as, "Time heals all wounds." Gently pressing for more detail, however, will frequently reveal a richer understanding of precisely what clients did to make changes in their lives.

Some clients are able to amplify exceptions, that is, identify differences, see what they did to make solutions happen, and so forth. In other cases, clients are less proficient at amplifying exceptions. And this serves as useful information as this might need to be a focus for tasks. After identifying and amplifying exceptions, the question arises as to what extent the exceptions represent an attainment of the goal. In other words, to what degree has the identification and amplification of exceptions bridged the gap between the problem and goal? I describe this evaluation process in detail in the next chapter. For now, let me note that in some cases, after the first session the counselor or client might consider that further sessions are not required to achieve the goal. In other cases, the goal might not have been fully reached, but it is agreed that the client has displayed sufficient movement in the direction of the goal, making further sessions unnecessary. At this point in the process, counselors proceed to the stage of reevaluating the problem (described in the next chapter). In most cases, however, it is agreed during the first session that further treatment is needed because more progress is required. Accordingly, the process shifts to the stage of coconstructing tasks.

COCONSTRUCTING TASKS

The stage of coconstructing tasks is aimed at clarifying and building on the problem, goal, exceptions, or potential exceptions that have already been identified. At the outset of this stage, the counselor can help carry the momentum from the previous stages by summarizing what has been discussed thus far. The summary should include reviewing with the client the problem and the goal that has been coconstructed and the exceptions that have been identified and amplified. It is also helpful to compliment the client at this time for taking the initiative to seek help and for his or her willingness to make positive changes.

Following is a list of five tasks that I most often use with clients and the corresponding rationales that guides my selection of the task. The descriptions and corresponding rationales of the tasks are followed by case examples that illustrate the application of each task. These are my favored solution-focused tasks. They represent a parsimonious attempt at establishing a decision tree from which to choose from a list of interventions aimed at realizing the objectives of solution-focused counseling. These tasks have been adapted from those developed by Molnar and de Shazer (1987) and have been extrapolated from over a decade of my own clinical experiences. In some cases, I deviate from the decision tree. In some instances, I might choose to not deliver a task at all. In other cases, I might select a task that is not listed here (see chapter 6 for other tasks and techniques), or I might create an entirely new task that is not listed in this book. I encourage readers to experiment in their own practices with the tasks I have described or to create their own tasks. Consider combining tasks and fitting tasks with clients and the unique circumstances of each case.

- *Task 1.* The client is told and asked, "Between now and the next time, I would like you to observe, so that you can tell me next time, about those times when you are able to make it (the goal) happen."

  Rationale: This task is given if the client is able to construct a problem and goal, and identify and amplify exceptions.

- *Task 2.* The client is told and asked, "Between now and the next time, I would like you to pay attention to and make note of what you do when you are able to effectively cope with or deal with the problem.

  Rationale: This task is given if the client is able to construct a problem and goal and identify exceptions, but is unable to amplify exceptions.

- *Task 3.* The client is told and asked, "Between now and the next time, I would like you to observe, so that you can tell me next time, what happens in your life (relationship, family, work situation) that you want to continue to have happen."

  Rationale: This task is given if the client is able to construct a problem and goal, and potential exceptions, but is unable to identify exceptions.

- *Task 4.* The client is told and asked, "Try to avoid making any drastic changes. If anything, think about what you will be doing differently when things are improved."

  Rationale: This task is given if the client is able to construct a problem, but is unable to construct a goal.

- *Task 5.* The client is told and asked, "The situation is very volatile. Between now and the next time, attempt to think about why the situation is not worse."

  Rationale: This task is given if the client is in severe crisis.

The aforementioned tasks and criteria are a parsimonious attempt at setting guidelines for the selection process. In some cases, more than one (if not all) of the tasks might be relevant to a client's situation. In other cases, it might be fitting to construct a different task or not to construct a task at all. In each case, it is critical for the task to make sense for the client and the client's situation. Accordingly, it is recommended that counselors suggest a task and then determine if the client agrees that it is a meaningful activity given the goal. Five case examples are provided to illustrate each of the tasks and the various stages of the solution-focused process.

Case 1

A 49-year-old woman presented with the problem of low self-confidence. The goal of increasing self-confidence was coconstructed. The client was asked to provide a video description of what would be happening when she reached this goal. The client stated that she would be more assertive with people (e.g., she would express her feelings in a direct manner). Various exceptions were identified and amplified. The client recalled, for example, that she had recently refused to loan money to a coworker. It was agreed that the client had demonstrated the ability to be assertive. At the end of the first session, we agreed on Task 1, and I told and asked the client, "Between now and the next time, I would like you to observe, so that you can tell me next time, about those times when you find that you are acting assertively."

Case 2

A man identified the problem as procrastination. He stated that he had a long history of procrastination, but was particularly troubled by his recent putting off of work responsibilities. He was a university professor and delayed many of his duties. As a result, he often missed deadlines and got himself into trouble. During the first session, several exceptions to his procrastination were identified. For example, over the past weekend he initiated a project without delay. The client was also able to identify other responsibilities that he met on time. The client was not, however, able to amplify these exceptions; that is, he was unsuccessful at noting differences between the times when he procrastinated and when he did not. Accordingly, the client and counselor agreed on Task 2. The client was told and asked, "Between now and the next time, I would like you to pay close attention to and make written notes of precisely how you did not procrastinate (i.e., what you did, what you were feeling, what you were thinking, what was happening, etc.)."

Case 3

A couple consensually defined the problem as a marriage that lacked excitement. The goal of increased excitement was coconstructed. The couple stated that there had been virtually no exciting times in the past year. They did agree that they had some excitement 6 months ago when they went to a party. The couple minimized this exception, however, maintaining that their marriage had otherwise been void of excitement. It was agreed that potential exceptions to the problem would be the couple's engaging in activities that might prove exciting, such as going to a party. At the end of the first session, we agreed on

Task 3, and I told and asked the couple, "Between now and the next time, I would like you both to observe, so that you can tell me next time, what happens in your marriage that represents even a small degree of excitement."

Case 4

A man defined the problem as depression. The client stated that he had been depressed for many years and for no apparent reason. Attempts to obtain a video description of the problem were unsuccessful as were efforts to coconstruct a goal. Accordingly, we agreed on Task 4, and I told and asked the client, "You have been dealing with this depression for some time now. I question whether or not you will ever find out how or why you got this way. I also doubt if it is necessary or preferable to find the cause or even if there is one. I suggest that you try to avoid making any significant changes. If you do anything, put some thought to what you will be doing differently when you are feeling less depressed."

Case 5

A 79-year-old man was referred by his primary care physician on an emergency basis. The client's wife of 45 years had died 2 weeks earlier. During the initial session, the client's mood was depressed, his affect was flat, and he admitted to having had death wishes since his wife's death. During the session, a thorough risk assessment was conducted which indicated that the client was not an imminent danger to himself. The client was encouraged to vent his feelings during the session. The client's sadness was normalized as part of the grief process. At the end of the session, we agreed on Task 5, and I told and asked the client, "There is no getting away from the fact that your loss is very painful. Given how much you say you loved your wife, I'm surprised that you're doing as well as you are. For now, I suggest that you give yourself permission to grieve and feel very sad."

CONCLUDING REMARKS

In this chapter, the clinical process followed during the first session in solution-focused counseling has been described. The clinical process is also applicable to second and subsequent sessions. At the end of the first session (and at the end of any session for that matter), I do not assume that there will be a next session. Accordingly, toward the end of every session, I usually ask the client, "Do you think we should reschedule?" Even if I think we should schedule another session, I ask this question to the client so that he or she can decide for him- or herself. I also do not assume when the next session shall be. Although it has become customary in our field to schedule sessions on a weekly basis, I do not necessarily follow this protocol. Sometimes I prefer to spread sessions out over the course of a few weeks to give clients an opportunity to practice the tasks we have agreed on. Finally, at the end of the session, I frequently write down the agreed-upon task, if there was one, as a reminder for the client.

CHAPTER 6

After the First Session

I t is usually preferable to maintain a focused approach with clients during the second and subsequent sessions in order to bring about significant change. Solution-focused counseling is brief by design, rather than brief by default (see chapter 1), because its practitioners recognize that most clients bring to counseling a readiness for change. This readiness for change might be missed if counselors do not remain focused after the first session and specifically help clients identify, highlight, and amplify exceptions. The main purposes of the second and subsequent sessions of solution-focused counseling are (a) identifying and amplifying exceptions derived from tasks, and identifying and amplifying exceptions that might have otherwise arisen in the client's life since the previous session; and (b) planning for termination of counseling by reevaluating the problem and goal; that is, determining the extent to which the exceptions represent an attainment of the client's treatment goals and if further sessions are still needed. In this chapter, I describe techniques used to facilitate purposes (a) and (b) during the second and subsequent sessions of solution-focused counseling.

IDENTIFYING AND AMPLIFYING EXCEPTIONS DERIVED FROM TASKS

It is important for counselors to demonstrate to the client at the outset of any follow-up session—especially the second session—that he or she remembers and is interested in what was previously discussed. Doing so will help both the client and the counselor remain focused. Accordingly, documentation that includes specific data corresponding to the solution-focused counseling process (including the problem, goal, exceptions, and amplifications) is essential, especially for those counselors who have large caseloads.

The session can be started by summarizing what was discussed during the previous session and reminding the client of the task. The main objective of any follow-up session in solution-focused counseling is to help the client identify and amplify exceptions. In particular, the counselor's job is to identify and amplify exceptions derived from tasks assigned in the previous session. Another objective of the follow-up session is to determine the extent to which the exceptions represent an attainment of the client's goal in counseling and if further treatment is still needed.

When identifying and amplifying exceptions, as in the first session, it is important for the counselor to use presuppositional language. This involves asking, "*What* has been happening that you want to continue have happening?" or "*What* did you notice that is a sign that things are going better?" as opposed to, "*Did* anything happen that you want to continue have happening?" or "*Did* you notice any signs of things that are going better?" If exceptions are identified, these should be amplified in the manner discussed in chapter 5. After amplifying exceptions, reevaluate the problem and goal (as discussed in this section).

If the client states, "I did not remember to do it (i.e., the task)," the counselor can avoid creating resistance and, instead, foster a cooperative approach by responding, "Okay. No problem. Let's think about it now. When was there a time this past week when you were dealing better with the problem?" In such cases, it is likely that the counselor will find him- or herself where he or she started in the previous session (i.e., in the early stage of initially identifying and amplifying exceptions). The client's not doing the task also serves as useful information for the counselor, namely, that perhaps this client will not be compliant with the type of task that was given. If the counselor wishes to enhance future cooperation from this client, then perhaps he or she had better modify tasks in the future to fit with this client or not give tasks at all to this client.

If the client reports that there were no exceptions, aim to identify small changes as described in chapter 5. If the client maintains that there were no exceptions, it may be necessary to reconstruct the problem or goal, or consider some of the techniques described later in this chapter. In some cases, however, exceptions come out later in the session (i.e., the client might recall exceptions after he or she stated that there were none). In other cases, especially with couples and families, clients will be very problem-focused at the start of follow-up sessions. They might assert that things got worse or they might have recently experienced a problematic situation (perhaps just before the session). When this happens, counselors can suggest to the client, "I am very interested in hearing about this, but I would first like to check on the task that we discussed at the end of the last session." Most of the time, clients will agree to this. After inquiring about the task (and hopefully identifying and amplifying exceptions), the problem can be reevaluated and, if needed, reconstructed. A couple, for example, came to the second session in a rage following a severe argument in the car on the way to the session. As the couple described the argument, I politely interrupted and inquired about how things had otherwise gone since the previous session. The couple recalled that it had been a great week. Thus, when clients are very problem-focused at this stage, counselors can attempt to divert their attention toward exceptions derived from the task, or they can join their clients in a problem focus and inquire about exceptions later.

When clients are stuck, the first thing I do is ask myself, "What can *I* do differently?" In keeping with solution-focused principles, a problem requires the doing of something different (de Shazer, 1991). Since I am a part of the treatment system, then I include myself in that which must change. Flexibility and imagination are key when it comes to dealing with such cases. I encourage readers to come up with their own innovative techniques when dealing with difficult clinical situations. Following are various techniques for overcoming roadblocks to change.

Do More of the Same

When I refer to "more of the same" here, I mean more of the exceptions. Sometimes clients are stuck simply because the counselor has given up too quickly on the basics of solution-focused counseling. Don't give up on it too quickly before shifting to another strategy or some other model. Did you carefully and patiently help the client to identify exceptions? Small exceptions? Potential exceptions? Did you amplify the exceptions? Perhaps you should give it another try. Maybe it would help to ask your questions differently. If you look back on your case notes, your client might have identified a small exception somewhere in the course of counseling but he or she—and you!—considered it to be irrelevant or unremarkable. Maybe you reinforced the client's view by not highlighting the exceptions.

Do Less of the Same

If the solution-focused approach seems to be getting you nowhere, you can shift to MRI's problem-focused model. I provided a description of MRI's theory of problem formation and change in chapter 3, so I will only briefly remind readers of its principles here. According to MRI, everyday life difficulties arise through the repeated application of ineffective solution attempts. When clients apply these ineffective solution attempts in a more-of-the-same manner, it can be said that the solution becomes the problem. The job of the counselor is to help clients interrupt the vicious cycle of ineffective problem-solving behavior through various techniques, including reframing and behavioral prescriptions.

Quick (1996) has developed an integration of the MRI and solution-focused models. I see the MRI and solution-focused models, however, as distinct approaches. Accordingly, I suggest that if you choose to follow a particular model, then do so faithfully. So if you are going to practice solution-focused counseling, then do not give up on it so quickly. I do not mean to suggest, however, that there is not a time and place for everything in counseling, and MRI's problem-focused model serves a useful purpose in cases when a solution-focused approach has becomes inadequate at resolving the client's problem and helping him or her attain his or her goal. The following case describes shifting from solution-focused counseling to MRI.

A single mother named Susan and her 14-year-old son Clinton came to counseling. During the first session, Susan identified the problem as Clinton's oppositional behavior. In particular, Susan stated that she and Clinton often got into power struggles. Susan also described Clinton as "an angry kid." Clinton was quiet for most of the session, and when he was called on to speak he had little to offer. Susan stated that her goal was to have more peace at home. She specified this goal as having fewer arguments with Clinton. Attempts at identifying and amplifying exceptions were unsuccessful. However, Susan was able to identify potential exceptions. For example, Susan stated that if a conflict arose, she and Clinton would be able to resolve the situation promptly and without a big argument or fuss. Accordingly, I asked Susan to do Task 3 (see chapter 5): "Between now and the next time, I would like you to observe, so that you can tell me next time, about times when you find that a conflict arises and you and Clinton are somehow able to resolve it without having as big an argument."

Susan came alone to the second session. She stated that she had a terrible week having had numerous arguments with Clinton. "Things are worse then ever," she told me. She also stated that Clinton had refused to come to the counseling session today. During the session, Susan described her long history of difficulties with Clinton. She then stated, "I know my son better than anyone else. And when we lock horns, I know that we are going to get into a struggle and that there is no winning." When Susan said this, my thinking shifted to MRI. The locking horns metaphor, which Susan introduced, helped me visualize a recursive, deviation-amplifying positive feedback loop (Fisch et al., 1982; Watzlawick et al., 1967, 1974). I thought to myself that if I could get Susan to back off while she and her son were locking horns, then perhaps this cycle would be interrupted during its most vicious and unproductive moments.

The biggest challenge for MRI counselors is to sell the behavioral tasks designed to interrupt or block clients' ineffective problem-solving behaviors. This is a challenge for counselors precisely because clients consider their ineffective solutions to be the best choices available to them given the current situation. It is therefore crucial to take into account the client's worldview when reframing the situation. In this case, I started by telling Susan, "You know your son better than anyone." This was the metaphor that Susan presented to me, so I used it. Her head was nodding in the affirmative. And then I simply suggested that since she knows him so well, perhaps when she sees that they are about to lock horns, that this is the very time for her to back off. "You said yourself..." I told her, "...that when this happens, there is no winning."

Susan came to the third session accompanied by Clinton. Both Susan and Clinton reported that it had been a good week. Susan recalled that in the past week there were two or three instances when she found that the two of them were about to lock horns. Each time, she reminded herself that there was no winning, so she unlocked herself from the struggle. It occurred to me that exceptions might have occurred as a result of this new pattern and that it might be worthwhile to shift back to solution-focused counseling at this juncture. So I asked Susan, "After you unlocked your horns, what did you and Clinton do that was effective to resolve your conflicts?" Various exceptions were identified and amplified, and I resumed my solution-focused approach.

Mapping the Influences of the Problem

Michael White (1988, 2000; M. White & Epston, 1990), in his narrative therapy model, has developed a technique called *mapping the influences of the problem* that I have adapted within solution-focused counseling. In narrative therapy, this technique refers to a line of questioning aimed at helping the client understand how the problem has influenced his or her life. This process serves to increase opportunities for identifying unique outcomes (a phenomenon that is similar to exceptions) and, also, externalize the problem by helping clients to view themselves as separate from the dominant stories (Foucault, 1987) that have contributed to their problems. When mapping the influences of the problem, counselors ask how the problem has affected various aspects of the client's life, including relationships, work, and daily functioning.

I do not use this technique in the same manner used by Michael White; that is, I do not emphasize the role of Foucault's (1987) dominant stories and the externalization process. Instead, I use this technique for other purposes. First, in cases when clients are very problem focused, I find that mapping the influences of the problem is a way to speak to their need to talk about the problem, address its influences, and feel as if the problem is not being stolen away from them. This is one of the downsides of a solution-focused approach and brief counseling models in general. Because brief counseling models are designed to produce such rapid results, some clients are left feeling as if the treatment is superficial. Mapping the influences of the problem can go a long way in addressing such concerns. If the problem is depression, then the counselor might ask the client to identify ways in which depression has affected aspects of his or her life. The counselor might ask, "How has the depression affected your work?" "How has the depression affected your relationships with family members?" or "How has the depression affected your health?" A second purpose of this technique is to use the influences as a basis from which to later identify exceptions. After the client has identified various influences of the problem, the counselor can go back to these influences and inquire about exceptions. In the case of anger, for example, the counselor might inquire about exceptions at work, in the client's relationships with family members, and with regard to his or her health.

What's Better?

De Shazer (1994) has proposed a simple question that counselors can use during follow-up sessions aimed at identifying exceptions: "What's better?" This is a good question to ask if you are unclear regarding where you left off after the prior session. Perhaps you did not agree on a task. Maybe it was unclear what the task would be. Maybe you and the client were unsure of what direction you were going in at the end of the prior session. Starting off the next session with the question, "What's better?" can get you and the client in a solution-focused direction from the start. This question might also help identify exceptions that were missed in prior sessions or raise new problems and exceptions that were never discussed before in counseling. There are many variations to the "What's better?" question. You can ask the client, "What's new?" You can even start the session with more neutral questions by asking, "What's up?" or "What do you want to talk about?"

Scaling Techniques

Many times clients understand the problem as an on/off experience (de Shazer, 1994). You either have it or you don't. Scaling techniques are useful for clients who find it difficult to discern exceptions and notice differences. Scales are useful because we can bypass the limitations of language and agree upon a term—for example, 6, 9, or 2—to denote what would otherwise be a subjective experience.

In solution-focused counseling, I ask clients to rate their subjective experiences, such as how they feel, how they deal with their problems, and so forth on a scale from 0 to 10. I adapted the system employed by Molnar and de Shazer (1987) in which they developed a reverse scale. Molnar and de Shazer have described the rationale for the use of this reverse system in the case of depression:

> The rating scale was deliberately upside-down. This was designed to help confuse the up-down metaphor and to have the shift from "depressed" (i.e., 7 or 8 ratings) to "normal" (2 or 1 ratings) be represented by a "downhill slide" rather than an "uphill battle." (p. 352)

I ask clients to keep a written record to keep track of their ratings. For example, for clients with anxiety, I might ask them to rate the severity of their anxiety on a daily basis. In addition, I ask them to record other information, such as what happened, what they did to cope, who they spent time with, and so forth. When we review the ratings, I focus on their best days and also highlight the other information that was recorded as these are exceptions that can be amplified.

The Structured Log

If you find yourself stuck in a case, you can always suggest that clients keep a structured log. Some clients prefer to use the term *journal* or *journaling* when referring to such activities. The structured log or journal is a useful exercise for clients who are unable to identify exceptions, are only able to identify potential exceptions, are not focused, are only able to construct vague goals, or are not able to develop goals at all. The client might be asked to keep track of times when the problem does not happen or when the goal happens. The client is asked to describe in detail what he or she did, how he or she coped, what was different, and so forth. For example, if a client describes the goal of counseling as "I want to be more in control of my life," he or she might be asked to keep a log of what he or she is doing when he or she finds him- or herself feeling more in control of life. Recalling that small changes can lead to big results, the client should be asked to make notes of any small examples, too. The structured log often leads to helping the client identify exceptions and set more attainable and realistic goals.

The Surprise Task

When I am working with couples and families, I sometimes use the surprise task (W. H. O'Hanlon & Weiner-Davis, 1989) to identify positive outcomes that might otherwise not have been produced in counseling. I tell the couple or family the following:

> Between now and the next time we meet, do at least two things that you think will surprise the other person (spouse, parent, or child). Do not tell them what the surprise is. The other person's task is to try and figure out what the surprise was. Be sure not to discuss the surprises between sessions. We will discuss them during our next session.

In this task, one family member (such as the husband) is instructed to surprise another family member on two occasions. The other family member (such as the wife) is instructed to observe for times when the other surprises him or her. The wife is therefore looking for surprises, similar to how clients are often guided to look for exceptions. In the next session, I usually begin by asking the other person (e.g., the wife) what surprises were observed. Usually, this other person reports more than two surprises. And often the person reports observing surprises that were not among those that the family member intended to be surprises.

Back to the Books

If the counselor intends to use an eclectic rather than generic approach (see chapter 3), then it is critical that he or she is educated in the model that is being introduced within solution-focused counseling. Remember that solution-focused counseling includes a strategic approach to eclecticism that allows for a basis from which to use divergent theories and techniques within the change process. There are essentially two scenarios in which counselors might find it appropriate to use an eclectic approach: (a) when clients initiate the presentation of clinical theories from other models (e.g., a client might be a previous consumer of some other theory and find utility in its principles); or (b) when the counselor considers that the theory or techniques might be helpful and, furthermore, that the approach is fitting with the client's worldview. In some instances, the counselor might have an adequate knowledge of the clinical system that is being incorporated within solution-focused counseling. For example, I have knowledge and experience in various models (e.g., REBT, behavior therapy) that do not require any remedial preparation on my part. There are other models, however, that would require some work on my part if I wish to include them in my counseling.

It is important for us to be educated in a breadth of models if we wish to adopt an eclectic approach to counseling. In keeping with solution-focused counseling's eclectic approach, the theories and techniques from other models are to be considered as metaphors (rather than objective representations of the domains of problems and change) that are used to realize the goals of our clinical system. Hence, it is not necessary to attain special expertise in any of these other theories in order to use them. But I urge counselors to dust off their textbooks and review each of the major systems of counseling and psychotherapy as well as the many less formal theories that have become the latest trends in our culture. Read self-help books from time to time, especially the best-sellers, if only to keep informed of what some of your clients are consuming.

When Less Is Better

Sometimes less is more. When I shared this insight with my father, a very wise man, he corrected me by pointing out that to say "less is more" feeds into the idea that size is important. "Instead…," my father suggested, "say, less is better." The following case illustrates an example of a less is better philosophy.

> A 56-year-old man named Jack was referred to counseling by his psychiatrist. Jack reported that his wife had died 5 years ago from cancer. His daughter died 1 year ago in a car accident. Since his daughter died, he had been grief stricken. His psychiatrist started him on an antidepressant. After experiencing limited results, his psychiatrist referred him to counseling. In the first session, Jack described his feelings of grief over the loss of his wife and daughter. Due to the client's painful affect and grief, I was reluctant to redirect Jack to focus on exceptions at such an early stage in counseling. Accordingly, I just listened, and we agreed to schedule a second session in 1 week.
>
> During the second session, Jack continued to express his feelings of loss. And I listened. I allowed Jack to express his grief while resisting my inclination to be solution-focused. Again, I offered no task at the end of the second session. We only agreed to meet again in 1 week.
>
> In the third session, Jack told me that he had derived a lot of benefit from being able to talk about his feelings in the counseling sessions. He said that he was normally a shy person who seldom expressed his feelings to anyone and that the counseling had been very helpful to him. It dawned on me that what had been transpiring in the counseling sessions—Jack's expressing his feelings in a safe environment—was in itself an exception

Mastering the Art of Solution-Focused Counseling

to the problem. The process that occurred in the counseling sessions was the solution. After about six sessions, Jack and I eventually shifted to a more active solution focus, but the minimalist approach I followed—the less is better philosophy—in the early stage of counseling went a long way in setting the stage.

Every client is different, and every case presents new challenges. So there is no formula for the minimalist approach just described. I have identified three guidelines, however, that counselors can follow when working toward a minimalist approach in solution-focused counseling:

1. *Slow down.* Often, counselors apply the solution-focused model in a mechanical way. Solution-focused counseling is not a machine. Remember that you are working with human beings who have real problems. Take your time. You will often find that you can reap the results of brief counseling in a shorter period of time if you go slow.
2. *Ask for more time.* Tell your client that you would like some time to think about his or her situation before jumping to any conclusions, and ask him or her to do the same. Be sincere about this. Tell your client that this is the first time that you are hearing about his or her problem and that you would like to have some more time to think about it. Be genuine about not knowing. Clients seem to appreciate such honesty and my willingness to think about their case between sessions.
3. *Summarize.* Simply recap what was discussed during the session. But do it well. Embellish your summary with a flair. Use the client's language. Highlight exceptions, strengths, and positives that were revealed during the session. Use humor when appropriate. Compliment the client for seeking help and any exceptions that were identified. Suggest that the session was time well spent.

Do Something Different

If all else fails, counselors need to try doing something different. De Shazer (1991) has defined *problem* as "anything that requires the doing of something" (p. 82). It follows that if counselors get stuck in their efforts to help clients solve their problems, then they (i.e., counselors) need to try different strategies if their favored methods are not working. Before abandoning one's chosen model, it is suggested that variations of the model be applied. It is for this reason that solution-focused counseling has developed a strategic approach to eclecticism. By doing so, it retains a solution-focused approach to process, yet allows for the inclusion of virtually any content. There might be instances when solution-focused counselors consider shifting to a different model altogether, and this might be the difference that makes a difference in some cases. In other cases, the counselor might be served well to seek supervision on a particularly difficult case. There is nothing to be ashamed about feeling stuck in a case and seeking help. Although I have over 20 years of clinical experience, I still feel stuck from time to time and regularly consult with colleagues about my work.

TERMINATING COUNSELING

Termination is an inevitable part of the counseling process. After identifying and amplifying exceptions, the problem and goal are reevaluated. If the goal has been reached or the client has made significant progress in the direction of the goal, then it might be appropriate for the counselor to ask the client at this time whether he or she thinks that further treatment is needed. I refer to this as "popping the question." Discussing with the client whether further treatment is needed maintains a focused approach during solution-focused counseling and helps curtail the incidence of dropouts. It seems that a large number of clients drop out of treatment after just a few sessions either by canceling or by just not showing for appointments (Kazdin, 1996). It has been suggested that some of these terminations are premature (Hatchett, 2004). From a social constructionist position, however, such an assumption represents an objectivist (i.e., independent of the observer) view pertaining to when treatment is and is not needed. Of course, there are instances when we feel responsible to intervene against clients' wishes (e.g., in cases when clients present as a danger to themselves or others), and our role as counselor is then transformed to that of social control agent (Boscolo, Cecchin, Hoffman, & Penn, 1987). Ideally, we should strive to reach a consensus with clients regarding the issue of when treatment is and is no longer needed.

If the client indicates that further treatment is still needed, this indicates that the problem and goal have not yet been satisfactorily resolved or attained, respectively. However, the client may also indicate that the goal has been reached and that there is now a new problem and goal. It could be said that talking about a problem at different times necessarily produces a change in its construction (i.e., the words used and, hence, the meaning ascribed to it changes). The counselor can use this inevitability to work toward reconstructing solvable problems. The goal might need to be more attainable, more general, more specific, or more relevant to the client's problem.

In cases when clients have made some gains in counseling yet feel that they have not made sufficient progress to end treatment, I find it helpful to enter into a discussion about how they might handle future problems. In particular, I ask clients how they might handle problems, conflicts, and challenges differently than they did in the past (W. H. O'Hanlon & Weiner-Davis, 1989). We review the specific strategies that clients are able to identify to deal with such situations (e.g., coping skills). These might be exceptions that have already been identified in counseling or they might take the form of potential exceptions. Then, I ask clients if they think they will be able to deal with these issues if they arise. If the client feels confident that he or she is able to deal with these issues, then I usually suggest that further sessions are no longer needed at this time. If the client agrees, then we terminate counseling. I always leave the door open and invite clients to reschedule an appointment in the future if they feel it is necessary. In some cases, clients report that they feel able to deal with their issues but still want to stay in counseling. Perhaps they feel that more progress is needed, they want to maintain the professional contact, they are not sure if their changes are for real, or they have other problems that they want to work on. In other cases, it seems clear that further counseling is still needed. The client might have made little progress toward the goal. Perhaps the goal is unattainable. If a client decides that the goal is to "be happy" and does not specify in behavioral terms what being happy is, then he or she is destined to fail.

Ideally, the counselor and client will reach a consensual agreement that additional sessions are no longer necessary because the goals of treatment have been met or sufficient progress has been made in the direction of the goal. In other cases, the decision to terminate is nonconsensual. The client simply drops out of treatment and disappears. Accordingly, I prefer to openly discuss termination issues at the outset of counseling in hopes of avoiding dropouts. I am confident that many clients drop out of counseling because they feel that the goals of counseling have been met. Unfortunately, this understanding was never communicated to the counselor. Discussing the inevitability of termination challenges counselors and clients to reevaluate, clarify, and redefine treatment goals. The ultimate goal in solution-focused counseling and counseling in general is to end treatment. If counselors are not proactive in making their treatment brief by design, then in many cases counseling will be brief by default.

CONCLUDING REMARKS

In this chapter, I have described techniques used during the second and subsequent sessions of solution-focused counseling. Most of these techniques are aimed at identifying and amplifying exceptions derived from tasks that were coconstructed in prior sessions. In addition, I have addressed terminating counseling, an inevitable stage of the treatment process. It has been suggested that discussing openly with the client whether further treatment is still needed maintains a focused approach during counseling and helps reduce dropouts. Finally, the main purpose of any session, especially the second and subsequent sessions, in solution-focused counseling is to help the client identify and amplify exceptions and thereby work toward treatment goals.

CHAPTER 7
Treating Depression

In this chapter, solution-focused applications to depression are described. Because many clients experience mild and moderate forms of depression, the principles in this chapter are presented so they can also be applied to less severe cases. Accordingly, this chapter provides guidelines for delivering solution-focused assessments, interventions, and tasks for depression along a continuum of severity and type. This chapter is organized as follows. First, a solution-focused approach to depression is described, including how this condition is conceptualized within solution-focused counseling. Next, solution-focused treatment strategies are presented. Then, a case example illustrates the application of the model to depression.

A SOLUTION-FOCUSED APPROACH TO DEPRESSION

It has been estimated that from 10% to 25% of the population has experienced some form of depression in their lifetimes (Paradise & Kirby, 2005). Moreover, depression is considered to be the primary cause of disability in the world (Murray & Lopez, 1997). Numerous studies have also suggested that depression is the most common disorder among people who seek mental health services (e.g., Gilroy, Carroll, & Murra, 2002). Hence, it is clear that depression is a serious and prevalent mental health problem. It is crucial, then, for counselors to be prepared for the inevitability that clients will present with complaints of depression and to develop effective clinical skills aimed at treating clients for this condition.

Various treatment approaches have been found to be effective for the treatment of depression, including medication, cognitive–behavioral therapy, and family counseling (Hollon, Thase, & Markowitz, 2002). In particular, an increasing literature supports the finding that brain abnormalities are causally related to depression and that medication is an effective and efficient approach to ameliorating depressive symptoms (e.g., Chilvers et al., 2001; Videbech,

Ravnkilde, & Fiirgaard, 2001). As a general rule, I refer clients to a psychiatrist for a medication evaluation if they meet the *DSM* criteria for a major depressive episode or major depressive disorder, for bipolar disorder, or if their mood symptoms significantly interfere with their daily functioning. Making a referral for a medication evaluation is a prevailing community standard of care when a client meets the *DSM* criteria for a major depressive episode, major depressive disorder, or bipolar disorder (Azocar, Cuffel, & Goldman, 2003), and hence, it is advisable for counselors to do so. I have also found that many severely depressed clients become more amenable to counseling interventions only after being placed on medication. This has become particularly apparent in solution-focused counseling, as severely depressed clients are often more likely to discern exceptions only after they have been on an antidepressant for a week or two.

In addition to biological theories of depression, numerous psychological theories have been set forth (e.g., learning, psychodynamic) as a basis from which to conceptualize and treat this disorder. Note that from a social constructionist and solution-focused perspective, these theories of depression are considered as *formal content*, that is, the counselor's assumptions regarding causation that are addressed across cases to solve problems (see chapter 3). Moreover, these formal contents are to be understood as metaphors rather than as objective representations of the domain of problem formation. This understanding sets the stage for a solution-focused conceptualization of depression.

Solution-Focused Conceptualization of Depression

If we accept the social constructionist position that we do not have access to clinical problems independent of the social interchange that occurs between counselors and clients, then it follows that problem definitions about depression are cocreated between counselors and clients. In keeping with solution-focused counseling's problem/exception ascription, depression is to be conceptualized as depressed/not depressed. In other words, the idea of depression necessarily begs the other side of the distinction, namely, times when the client is not depressed. Molnar and de Shazer (1987) have illustrated a solution-focused conceptualization of depression by way of the following case example:

> Mr. G., a 25-year-old man, came to therapy complaining that, "I have been depressed all my life." The therapist asked, "How do you know you're depressed?" Mr. G. described feeling unsatisfied with his job performance, his friendships, his marriage, his relationship with his family, etc. Nothing seemed O.K. to him and he could recollect no time in his life when he did not feel depressed. The therapist asked him again, "So, since you've been that way all your life, how do you know you are feeling depressed and those feelings are not normal?" Mr. G. then mentioned "occasional 'up-days'" as examples of how he knew that he was depressed on the other days. To Mr. G., these 'up-days' were flukes, chance events which did not change his idea that he had been depressed all his life. (pp. 351–352)

"Depression" is inextricably linked to storytelling and language. This is obvious in everyday life, in popular culture, and in the daily clinical practices of counselors. Accordingly, a starting point in solution-focused counseling is to understand depression in terms of the stories that clients and counselors tell. An increasing literature has also addressed the important role of cultural issues in the assessment, diagnosis, and treatment of depression (e.g., Kress, Eriksen, Rayle, & Ford, 2005; Marsella & Kaplan, 2002). In the *DSM–IV–TR*, it is suggested that "culture can influence the experience and communication of symptoms of depression" (APA, 2000, p. 353). The *DSM–IV–TR* includes an outline for cultural formulation designed to assist clinicians in assessing the impact of clients' cultural contexts and, also, a glossary of 25 culture-bound syndromes for use with diverse clients. The term *shenjing shuairuo*, for example, is a syndrome specific to China that is "characterized by physical and mental fatigue, dizziness, headaches, other pains, concentration difficulties, sleep disturbance, and memory loss" (p. 902). Some critics have cautioned, however, that the *DSM*'s glossary of culture-bound syndromes is hardly exhaustive and, moreover, is limited to the extent to which it accounts for differences that exist between and within cultures (Guarnaccia & Rogler, 1999; Kress et al., 2005; Thakker, Ward, & Strongman, 1999). It is important to also account for the client's unique worldview in the diagnostic process (Lonner & Ibrahim, 2002).

In solution-focused counseling, it can be said that the client and counselor coconstruct their understandings of depression in a special conversation. This way of conceptualizing depression is not meant to minimize the lived experiences of depression for our clients. Rather, it is meant to place the locus of the problem in the very language system that the client and the counselor are a part. Some people, as in the case example of Mr. G, tell tales of being depressed for all their lives. It is not uncommon for a client to say, "I am *always* depressed." In the case example of Mr. G., the counselor shifted the conversation to a solution focus with a single question: "How do you know you're depressed?" The power of this question was nontrivial because it forced the client to think about times when he was not depressed (i.e., exceptions). In solution-focused counseling, it is theorized that depression maintains itself largely because the client views it as always happening. The theory of change in solution-focused counseling holds that if the client is able to identify and amplify exceptions to the problem, then he or she will make a profound inversion (i.e., the exceptions will become the rule).

Either a generic or eclectic approach can be followed in the solution-focused counseling treatment of depression. In some cases, it might be fitting to follow a generic approach, that is, to coconstruct an understanding of depression that is void of any reference to formal content. In other cases, some counselors might find it helpful to use an eclectic approach to conceptualizing and intervening in relation to the problem. In yet other cases, clients might find value in attributing some cause (i.e., formal content) to their depression. The counselor and the client might find it helpful to use theories and techniques from other clinical systems for psychoeducational and skill-building purposes. For example, I frequently incorporate theories and techniques from Ellis's (1996a) REBT, Beck's (1976) cognitive therapy, and Meichenbaum's (1977) cognitive–behavior modification as well as numerous other formal clinical approaches. In addition, solution-focused counseling can often be supplemented by encouraging clients to use self-help resources.

Sudden Gains in Depression

Recent research has begun to pay more attention to a phenomenon called *sudden gains* in the context of counseling and psychotherapy (Tang & DeRubeis, 1999; Tang, Luborsky, & Andrusyna, 2002). In contrast to the commonly held view that clients improve gradually and slowly over the course of treatment, this research has shown that many clients experience significant improvements quickly, suddenly, and often in one *between-session* interval. Several important conclusions have been drawn regarding sudden gains. It has been suggested that sudden gains can trigger an "upward-spiral" that contributes to clients eventually coming out of depression (Tang & DeRubeis, 1999). In addition, it has been found that sudden gains tend to be occasioned by critical events in treatment in which substantial cognitive changes occur (Tang et al., 2002).

Research in the area of sudden gains holds promise for crystallizing our understanding of what transpires during change processes in the solution-focused treatment of depression and other clinical problems as well. In solution-focused counseling, it is theorized that clients have preexisting coping skills, strengths, and resources (i.e., exceptions) that play a critical role in reducing depressive symptoms. It is assumed that if these exceptions are identified and amplified, then marked shifts in the client's thinking about his or her depression will occur. The client's sudden cognitive shift to exceptions often contributes to an upward spiral whereby significant improvement can transpire suddenly and unexpectedly. The change processes in solution-focused counseling can therefore be likened to the phenomenon of sudden gains (Tang & DeRubeis, 1999; Tang et al., 2002) insofar as significant progressions on the part of clients are not to be considered as chance events or flights into health. Rather, these events are expectable progressions that derive from solution-focused interventions.

In order for solution-focused counseling to be effective in the treatment of depression, it is crucial for counselors to (a) recognize that sudden gains are inevitable and (b) assist clients in actualizing these sudden gains. A starting point for (a) is for counselors to take a not-knowing position and join the client in the process of coconstructing the problem and goal. Doing so allows counselors to consider possibilities for solutions that might have otherwise been missed had they taken a more traditional, modernist perspective. Not knowing is not easy given the a priori assumptions regarding depression that counselors frequently bring to counseling. Experienced and new counselors alike often search for—*and find!*—some formal content on the basis of their view that there is some real cause to depression. Counselors assume that unless this objectively defined cause is identified and addressed, the client will not get to the root of the problem, and therefore significant problem resolution will not occur. Sadly, this effort to get to the real cause of depression on the part of counselors often interferes with (b), that is, identifying and amplifying exceptions and thereby actualizing sudden gains.

TREATMENT STRATEGIES FOR DEPRESSION

The treatment of depression in solution-focused counseling begins with the process of coconstructing a problem definition and goal. In some respects, every case in solution-focused counseling is different. In other respects, every case is the same. Every case is different because each client offers a unique story (i.e., informal content) about the problem. Each case is similar, however, insofar as this unique informal content is then subsumed within solution-focused counseling's problem/exception ascription (i.e., formal content). Various assessment methods can be followed for the treatment of depression. Counselors can follow either a generic or an eclectic approach to solution-focused counseling so long as the chosen informal content fits with the client's worldview.

Counselors might also find it helpful to *map the influences of the problem* (see chapter 6) for depression, especially in cases when clients are very problem focused and feel a need to process their stories at length. As mentioned in chapter 6, mapping the influences of the problem serves as a basis from which to later identify exceptions. After the client has identified various influences of the problem, the counselor can later refer to these influences and inquire about exceptions. In cases of depression, the counselor might inquire about times when the client has experienced improvement in his or her mood at work, while participating in recreational activities or in the context of relationships, and so forth.

There seem to be no unequivocal guidelines for cocreating a problem and goal for depression in solution-focused counseling beyond looking to the client for direction. A principal question is how to go about cocreating an understanding of depression that is solvable. As in all phases of solution-focused counseling, it is important to develop goals in positive (rather than negative) language (i.e., as an increase of something, rather than as a decrease of something). The goal of decreasing depression, then, would not allow for a clear picture of the desired outcome. In contrast, the goal of increasing effective coping skills for depression is stated in positive terms. The process of goal setting for depression can also be specified by asking clients to provide video descriptions of the problem. Constructing a problem and a goal that fits with the client's worldview is also among the most important criteria during this phase of solution-focused counseling. In particular, it is critical to develop an understanding that takes into account the client's unique cultural background.

Identifying and Amplifying Exceptions

After coconstructing a problem and goal in relation to depression, the counselor shifts to the process of identifying and amplifying exceptions. This is perhaps the principal technique in solution-focused counseling. Readers are referred to chapter 5 for a thorough review of this process and, in particular, the *amplifying questions* that are used during this stage of treatment. It is reminded that questions aimed at identifying and amplifying exceptions are presuppositional insofar as they are to be considered interventions in themselves. In the case of depression, a client might be asked, "*When* has there been a time during the past week when you did something to cope better with the depression?" This question is interventive because it is designed to produce a sudden shift in the client's problem focus. If the client is able to identify an event in response to this question, then the counselor proceeds to amplify the exception. For example, the counselor might ask, "How did you make that happen?" This question is designed to create a context for establishing a sense of self-efficacy for the client.

During this stage of treatment, counselors might attempt to identify and amplify multiple exceptions to depression. In some cases, numerous exceptions will be identified. In other cases, only one or several exceptions will be revealed. In some instances, clients might struggle to amplify exceptions. Again, each case is different, yet in some respects, each case is the same. In chapter 5, guidelines are provided for responding to various scenarios with regard to the client's efforts to identify and amplify exceptions. For example, if the client states that there have been no exceptions, encourage the client to consider small differences. If clients are altogether unable to identify exceptions, then help them to identify potential exceptions. Questions aimed at identifying potential exceptions might take the form of asking, "What will it be like when you are coping better with the depression?"

The Miracle Question

The miracle question invites clients to view themselves in a future situation in which they are functioning satisfactorily (de Shazer, 1988). In cases when clients are unable to identify exceptions to depression, the following question can be asked to identify potential exceptions:

> "Suppose that one night there is a miracle and while you are sleeping the depression was resolved. How would you know? What would be different?"

The miracle question is an effective intervention for depression because it encourages clients to shift their focus from what is not working to what is possible. As mentioned in chapter five, it is important to ask the miracle question in a way that fits with the client's worldview. Some clients are so depressed that they are simply not ready to be asked about a miracle. It's too positive. When I do ask the so-called miracle question to a depressed client, I prefer to do so in less optimistic terms. So I might ask the client, "How would the depression be if it was going a little better?"

Coconstructing Tasks

Coconstructing a task is aimed at clarifying and building on the problem, goal, exceptions, or potential exceptions that have already identified in relation to depression. In chapter 5, I set forth a list of five tasks that I most often use with clients and the corresponding rationales that guide my selection of the task. These tasks represent an attempt at establishing a decision tree from which to choose from a list of interventions aimed at realizing the objectives of solution-focused counseling. All of the five tasks described in chapter 5 are applicable to depression. In some cases, however, I deviate from the decision tree. I might select a task that is not listed among the five tasks (see chapter 6 for other tasks and techniques) or I might create an entirely new task that is not listed in this book. Nevertheless, I have found that the five tasks listed in chapter 5 can often be tailored to the unique aspects of each client and realize the goals of a solution-focused approach.

Following is a list of the five tasks that I most often use with depressed clients and the corresponding rationales that guides my selection of the task.

- *Task 1.* The client is told and asked, "Between now and the next time, I would like you to observe, so that you can tell me next time, about those times when you are able to cope more effectively with the depression."

  Rationale: This task is given if the client is able to construct a problem and goal, and identify and amplify exceptions.

- *Task 2.* The client is told and asked, "Between now and the next time, I would like you to pay attention to and make note of what you do when you are able to effectively cope with the depression.

  Rationale: This task is given if the client is able to construct a problem and goal and identify exceptions, but is unable to amplify exceptions.

- *Task 3.* The client is told and asked, "Between now and the next time, I would like you to observe, so that you can tell me next time, what happens in your life (relationship, family, work situation) that is a sign of improvement in relation to the depression."

  Rationale: This task is given if the client is able to construct a problem and goal, and potential exceptions, but is unable to identify exceptions.

- *Task 4.* The client is told and asked, "Try to avoid making any drastic changes. If anything, think about what you will be doing differently when things are improved."

  Rationale: This task is given if the client is able to construct a problem, but is unable to construct a goal.

- *Task 5.* The client is told and asked, "The situation is very volatile. Between now and the next time, attempt to think about why the situation is not worse."

  Rationale: This task is given if the client is in severe crisis.

Scaling Techniques

Clients frequently experience depression as a constant in their lives. Statements such as "I am always depressed" or "I have been depressed all of my life" reflect this sort of experience. Accordingly, many clients understand depression as an on/off experience. You either have depression or you don't. Scaling techniques (see chapter 6) can help create a shift in this either/or type of thinking. Scaling techniques can be used as a supplement to the tasks described in the preceding section. Scaling is also often an integral part of the assessment process during solution-focused counseling sessions and then becomes an intervention in itself.

Scaling techniques are particularly useful when clients find it difficult to discern difference and thereby identify exceptions. Even the most severely depressed person has days when he or she is a little less depressed. In solution-focused counseling, it is assumed that these "less depressed" days are exceptional and hold the key to the development of a solution. Sometimes scaling is the most efficient method from which to uncover these exceptions. Scaling is effective because it avoids the limitations of language and, instead, employs quantifiable terms to denote what would otherwise be subjective experiences.

I usually ask clients to rate their depression on an upside-down version of a scale from 0 to 10 (Molnar & de Shazer, 1987). The rating scale is deliberately reversed to confuse the usual up-down metaphor, which tends to produce an uphill battle. In this upside-down version, a rating of 10 refers to *depressed* and 0 refers to *normal*. Hence, progress takes the form of a downward slide. I might ask a client to rate the severity of his or her depression on a daily basis and also request that the client record other information, including what happened, what he or she did to cope, who he or she spent time with, and so forth. The scaling technique can be conducted during sessions or as a task between sessions. The purpose of reviewing these ratings is to focus on the days with the lowest ratings and thereby identify and amplify exceptions. I often encourage clients to use a written form to record the daily scales. The use of a form is helpful because it serves to remind clients to do the task. In addition, a form can include instructions for following the upside-down version of the 0 to 10 scale, which is often confusing to clients and counselors alike. The use of a written form to record clients' daily scaling ratings makes the results real insofar as it provides evidence to support the client's progress.

Other Techniques

Numerous techniques can be effectively used in a solution-focused approach to depression. A general rule of thumb is to assess that any given technique fits the goal of counseling that has been agreed on between the client and the counselor. Some clients might wish to eliminate the depression, whereas others might accept depression as a part of their lives and instead choose to cope with the condition. In most cases, however, it is necessary for clients to counteract their depressive symptoms with behavioral action. Accordingly, activity tasks are usually a common assignment. Clients can be asked to keep a structured log or journal to schedule and monitor activities. The scaling technique can be also used along with logs or journals as a means to assess progress. Solution-focused counseling's strategic eclecticism also provides a basis from which to consider a wide selection of techniques for depression. If an eclectic rather than generic approach is used for the treatment of depression, then it is important that counselors be educated in the model that is employed. Self-help resources might also serve as useful content during the change process.

DOUBLE TROUBLE: A CASE EXAMPLE

Following is a case example that illustrates the application of solution-focused counseling to depression. A 33-year-old White married female named Lisa was self-referred for counseling. Lisa had been married for 5 years and she had no children. She reported that she had suffered from chronic depression for as long as she could remember. Lisa stated that she was diagnosed with dysthymia approximately 10 years ago. Upon conducting a comprehensive psychosocial history and a thorough mental status examination, the counselor found that the client met the *DSM* criteria for dysthymia with superimposed major depression. Lisa had been prescribed various antidepressants through the years with limited effectiveness. She also reported that on one occasion she had been in a psychiatric hospital following an intentional overdose of pills. Lisa added that she had tried therapy and counseling on numerous occasions in the past, but none of it had ever seemed to help. The following excerpt illustrates the counselor and client working together at the start of the first session to coconstruct a problem and goal in relation to the depression.

> *Counselor:* What do you think would be a good place for us to start?
> *Client:* Maybe with other people.
> *Counselor:* Okay. Can you explain that to me?
> *Client:* I think that other people have a problem with me.
> *Counselor:* They have a problem?
> *Client:* Yes.
> *Counselor:* Okay.
> *Client:* They are the ones with the problem.
> *Counselor:* Okay. Let's talk about that.
> *Client:* They have a problem.
> *Counselor:* Let's talk about how other people have a problem.
> *Client:* The depression. I, you know, have a problem, you know. I see that.
> *Counselor:* Right.
> *Client:* I'm not saying it's not a problem or anything.
> *Counselor:* Okay.
> *Client:* But I think a lot of it is that people around me think it is a really big issue.
> *Counselor:* Okay.
> *Client:* Right.
> *Counselor:* Can you give me an example?

Client: My husband. My husband and my mother, actually. Basically, they are both always on my case.

Counselor: Can you describe to me what happens when they get on your case?

Client: Oh, it's hell. My mother is always calling me up and asking me, "How do you feel?" And my husband yells at me. He yells at me. Like, "Get up. Do something already." He thinks he is trying to help, but he makes it worse. They treat me like a child.

Counselor: And when your mother or your husband do those things, how does it make *you* feel?

Client: More depressed. Guilt.

Counselor: Okay. Can you tell me more about your mother or your husband being on your case?

Client: Sure. And it's not only them. It's friends. Almost anybody. It can even be me.

Counselor: Now what do you mean it can even be you?

Client: I get on my case, too.

In this excerpt, the client initiated an understanding of the problem in terms of how other people respond to her depression and how she responds to her own depression. Hence, the client's understanding of the problem took the form of a perspective that was meta to the depression itself; that is, coping with other peoples' negative responses to her depression rather than the depression itself. According to the client, these negative responses contributed to an exacerbation of her depression. For example, the client stated that she feels more depressed when her husband gets on her case. The counselor spent much of the first session attempting to gain an understanding of the client's view of the problem. A good deal of the first session also involved mapping the influences of the client's problem definition. For example, the client stated that she frequently responded negatively to her depression which, in turn, made her feel more depressed and guilty.

Counselor: Tell me more about what you do in response to the depression.

Client: Oh, I hate myself. I get on my own case. I give myself a hard time.

Counselor: Sort of like what your mother and husband do.

Client: Yeah. Same thing.

Counselor: And what happens when you do that to yourself?

Client: It makes it worse. I get more depressed. I feel guilty.

Counselor: Is it kind of like you are depressed about being depressed?

Client: Exactly!

Counselor: Okay. So it's double trouble.

Client: Exactly! It's double trouble. I can deal with the depression. I've had it all my life.

Counselor: Okay.

Client: It's the second part I can't deal with. I can deal with the depression. It's the second part I want to deal with.

Counselor: The being depressed about being depressed. And the guilt about being depressed.

Client: Yeah.

Counselor: And that seems to come mainly from the pressure you get from people.

Client: Yeah.

Counselor: Pressure from other people to get over the depression.

Client: Right.

Counselor: And the sense I get from you is that some of that pressure, perhaps a good deal of that pressure, is coming from you. You put a lot of pressure on yourself to not be depressed.

Client: I do.

The client and counselor agreed to a consensual problem definition, namely, the pressure that people place on the client (including the client herself) to not be depressed. The counselor and client agreed to work on the goal of improving her coping skills for the secondary symptoms (e.g., feeling depressed, guilty) about her primary symptom of depression. Time did not permit the counselor and client to identify exceptions during the first session. Accordingly, the following task, a version of Task 4 (see chapter 5), was delivered to the client at the end of the first session: "Between now and the next session, think about what you will be doing differently when you are coping more effectively with the pressure that other people and you place on you about being depressed." The counselor began the second session by following up on the task that was given at the end of the first session.

Counselor: At the end of last session, I asked you to think about what you will be doing differently when you are coping better with the pressure. So let me ask you now. What have you come up with in the past week?

Client: I've been doing a lot of thinking.

Counselor: Good.

Client: I realized that a good place to start is with me.

Counselor: You came up with that idea?

Client: Yeah.

Counselor: That's an incredible idea.

Client: Yeah. I realized that if I can deal with it, then I am able to deal with other people.

Counselor: Wow. You came up with that idea?

Client: Yeah.

Counselor: That's an incredible idea.

Client: Thanks.

Counselor: So what have you done to try this out? To not put as much pressure on yourself about the depression?

Client: Accept it.

In this excerpt, the client began to verbalize insight or awareness that she has attained about her problem since the previous session. The client stated, "I realized that a good place to start is with me." The counselor then attempted to identify an exception that might exemplify the client's new insight by asking, "So what have you done to try this out?" Following the client's response, "Accept it," the counselor attempted to identify exceptions in behavioral terms. The client stated that during the past week she had changed her thinking in significant ways. In the past, the client frequently felt guilty and blamed herself for being depressed. During the past week, however, the client reported that she experienced a sudden change in her thinking.

Client: All of my life I have worried about other people. And I'm tired of it.

Counselor: I see.

Client: So I've been doing some thinking.

Counselor: So help me understand precisely what this thinking is. What are you thinking now?

Client: When I said last time that I wanted to start with me, I meant it. So I decided to stop blaming myself for being depressed. That's it, basically.

Counselor: That's it.

Client: Yeah.

Counselor: Yeah. Well, but that's a lot. How did you do that?

Client: How did I do that?

Counselor: Yeah. Because I think this is the kind of thing we were talking about in terms of you putting less pressure on yourself.

Client: It is.

Counselor: So can you tell me how you did that? How did you stop blaming yourself?

Client: I just did it, I guess. I don't know.

Counselor: Okay. That's fine. But if we could, do you mind if we just look at this more closely for a moment to see if we can figure it out? I am asking you this because understanding what you did might help.

Client: Sure.

Counselor: I suspect that you went through a thinking process. For our purposes we could say that you began a conversation with yourself. It might have started by your saying to yourself something like, "I am not to blame for being depressed." Or maybe that thought or a variation of it came later in the conversation.

Client: Yeah. It was kind of like that.

Counselor: Okay. So can you tell me what the conversation was like for you?

Client: Well, it's hard to put into words.

Counselor: Sometimes it's easier to go with feelings.

Client: I was saying that even though I have depression, I am a good person. So I don't have to blame myself. It's that simple.

Counselor: It's that simple. It is.

Mastering the Art of Solution-Focused Counseling

Client: And then, if other people are upset or treat me weird, that is their problem. At least I am not going to blame myself. That's the thing. I can let them to do their thing, but I'm going to be less upset than they are about me.

Counselor: I think I understand. So we have you, a person who is depressed. And other people, say, your mother, your husband, respond in ways that might have upset you in the past.

Client: Yes.

Counselor: In the past you have put pressure on yourself to not be depressed, and as a result, you have blamed yourself for being depressed and then you felt guilty.

Client: Exactly!

Counselor: Then, when these other people responded negatively to your condition, you reacted by blaming yourself even more. These other people placed pressure on you to not be depressed and this sort of reinforced the pressure that you were placing on yourself.

Client: Exactly! But I made a decision to let go.

Remember that the coconstructed problem in this case was the pressure that people placed on the client (including the client herself) to not be depressed. The agreed-upon goal of counseling was improving the client's coping skills for the secondary symptoms (e.g., feeling depressed, guilty) about her depression. In the preceding excerpt, the counselor attempted to identify the specific change in the client's thinking that contributed to her putting less pressure on herself about being depressed. In the preceding excerpt, the client stated, "So I decided to stop blaming myself for being depressed. That's it, basically." This decision on the part of the client is an exception insofar as it represents an effective coping skill for the coconstructed problem. The counselor then helped the client amplify this exception by asking, "How did you do that?" One of the main purposes of amplifying exceptions is to help clients discern differences between the times when the problem is happening and times when it is not. Once clients are able to identify how they were able to make exceptions happen, they will know what it will take to maintain their progress. Later in the session, the counselor asked additional amplifying questions. In particular, the counselor asked, "Who else noticed this change in your attitude?" This is a variation of the amplifying question, "Who else noticed?" (see chapter 5) and is designed to help clients identify exceptions that might otherwise not have been considered. This question was especially relevant to this case because the coconstructed problem and goal were organized around how other people reacted to the client's depression. According to the client, very little had changed in the past week in terms of how her mother and husband had responded to her, but the client reported feeling less vulnerable to their responses as a result of her new attitude. More specifically, the client reported that she was more tolerant of herself and thereby found it easier to be more tolerant of the negative responses of other people.

The counselor and client met for regular counseling sessions over the course of the next 3 months. Eventually, the problem and goal of counseling were clarified. The client's attention moved away from the reactions of other people in relation to her depression and, instead, was more focused on how she responded to her depression. This shift seemed fitting to both the counselor and client because as the client demonstrated an increased tolerance of herself, she found that she was able to be more tolerant of others' responses to her. As counseling progressed, the client also reported a significant decrease in her primary symptoms of depression, although this was not necessarily a principal goal of treatment.

CONCLUDING REMARKS

Depression is a common and serious mental health problem, and it has become increasingly important for counselors to develop effective treatment approaches for this condition. In this chapter, solution-focused applications to depression have been described.

Solution-focused counseling holds promise as an effective treatment approach for depression. In addition, the model has the potential to help theorists, researchers, and practitioners gain a better understanding of the phenomenon of sudden gains in relation to depression and other clinical problems (Tang & DeRubeis, 1999; Tang et al., 2002). Accordingly, it suggests that future research could assess outcome effectiveness related to solution-focused applications to depression.

CHAPTER 8
Substance Problems

I n this chapter, I describe the application of solution-focused counseling to substance problems. First, a solution-focused approach to substance problems is described, including how this condition is conceptualized in solution-focused counseling. Then, I consider treatment strategies. Finally, I present a case example that illustrates the application of the model.

A SOLUTION-FOCUSED APPROACH TO SUBSTANCE PROBLEMS

It is clear that substance abuse is a widespread problem for people and society. Suggesting that there are alternatives to traditional substance abuse treatment models is an emotionally charged issue in some professional circles. The prevailing substance abuse treatment approaches have long been the disease model and 12-step programs, and even the thought of deviating from these models is sure to raise eyebrows among their proponents. When Berg and Miller (1992) published their book, *Working With the Problem Drinker: A Solution-Focused Approach*, it was considered to be heretical by some traditionalists. Since Berg and Miller's book was published, however, there has been a proliferation of solution-focused approaches to substance abuse and addiction (e.g., Mason, Chandler, & Grasso, 1995; Pichot, 2001).

Solution-Focused Conceptualization of Substance Problems

From a solution-focused perspective, substance abuse is like any other clinical problem insofar as the focus is on clients' existing strengths, resources, and problem-solving skills. Indeed, clients with substance problems present counselors with unique challenges. But if the fundamental principles of solution-focused counseling are applied, then these clients can be helped in effective ways. So I refer readers to previous chapters in this book for a review of the basics in the theory and practice of solution-focused counseling. I also invite readers to consider how the basic principles of solution-focused counseling might be applied in creative and innovative ways to help clients who are experiencing substance problems.

In solution-focused counseling, the focus in substance abuse treatment is on what the client is doing right, rather than on his or her deficits, problems, or weaknesses. In keeping with the process outlined in chapter 5, the counselor works with the client to identify exceptions to the problem (e.g., times when the client is able to abstain from using). Then these exceptions are amplified through a series of interventive questions. Examples of questions aimed at amplifying exceptions for substance problems include the following:

1. How did you abstain from using?
2. What did you do instead of using?
3. What else did you do that helped you abstain?
4. What does this say about your ability to cope with urges to use in the future?
5. What are the possibilities?

The following case describes the use of solution-focused counseling with a 42-year-old man who reports he had relapsed on cocaine. The man, who described a long history of cocaine abuse, self-referred to counseling after he had used cocaine the night before.

> *Counselor:* Tell me about the times when you have been able to manage the cocaine problem, when you have been able to stay off it for an extended period of time?
> *Client:* I went to NA [Narcotics Anonymous] meetings.
> *Counselor:* NA meetings.
> *Client:* Yeah.
> *Counselor:* And that worked for you?
> *Client:* Yeah.
> *Counselor:* And how often did you go?
> *Client:* Oh, different times, depending on how I felt. Sometimes once a week. Sometimes more. Sometimes every day.

The counselor's question, "Tell me about the times when you have been able to manage the cocaine problem, when you have been able to stay off it for an extended period of time?" is designed to identify exceptions and get the client back on track after his relapse. The client was able to identify an exception, attending NA meetings.

> *Counselor:* What else have you done in the past to stay clean?
> *Client:* I stayed busy.
> *Counselor:* Tell me more about that.
> *Client:* Just staying busy. Staying out of trouble.

Mastering the Art of Solution-Focused Counseling

Counselor: What kind of things did you do?

Client: Besides meetings?

Counselor: Yes.

Client: I would do things, like go out with my family or do stuff around the house.

Counselor: And how did that help?

Client: It kept my mind off drugs.

The counselor's question, "What else have you done in the past to stay clean?" is designed to identify additional exceptions. The client identified an additional exception, staying busy. Although the client was unable to provide an example of staying busy at first, the counselor helped him do so through a careful line of questioning. Eventually, the client identified family and household activities as examples of keeping busy. The counselor's question, "And how did that help?" is meant to amplify this exception.

At the end of the session, the client felt that he was able to remain clean and resume his previous solutions. He stated that he intended to attend NA meetings regularly and stay busy. The counselor and client agreed to schedule a follow-up session in 1 week. At the follow-up session, the client reported that he had remained clean and was attending NA meetings on a daily basis. It was agreed that counseling was no longer needed, but the counselor invited the client to schedule another appointment in the future should the need arise.

Focus on Small Changes

Note that a small change is often all that is needed to start the ball rolling in the direction of change. As mentioned in chapter 1, taking the first step is important because it often takes an extra effort—a sudden burst of activity—and these exceptional events should be identified and highlighted in counseling. Once these small changes are discerned, however, sometimes the best thing that counselors can do is get out of the way. A case example provided by Berg and Miller (1992) makes the point:

> A 54-year-old self-described "alcoholic" male entered treatment a few days following a 2-month long "relapse". . . . The man described a life-long history of problems with alcohol and multiple treatment failures. Discouraged by his relapse, he thought he needed to stay in a 28-day inpatient treatment facility in which he had been placed. He responded to an inquiry about those times when he had successfully managed his problems with alcohol, noting lengthy periods (e.g., months, years) during which he had successfully managed his problems with alcohol. When queried in more detail, he was able to specify what he had done differently during those times that contributed to his success. Among a host of other things, he indicated that he attended at least a few AA [Alcoholics Anonymous] meetings a week. Thereafter, the man was asked what it would take to begin doing more of what had previously worked. He expressed

relatively high confidence that he could at least begin doing some of those things (e.g., attending a few AA meetings). The man was released from the hospital the day after the initial meeting. Over the course of two subsequent treatment sessions, this simple strategy was employed to create the opportunity for a solution to develop. Just recently, the man sent a copy of his 1-year sobriety token from Alcoholics Anonymous to the therapist. When asked during a congratulatory phone call about what had been helpful about his treatment, he replied, "You got me started and then you got the hell out of my way!" (p. 11)

Abandon the Concepts of Resistance and Denial

When working with substance problems, most cases do not turn out to be as successful as the one previously described. Many factors contribute to failure in substance treatment. Many counselors attribute such treatment failures to "resistance" or "denial" on the part of the client. From a solution-focused perspective, however, such labels give us more information about counselors than clients. So-called resistance and denial are better understood as byproducts of the client–counselor relationship rather than as something that exists inside of the client. This understanding can go a long way in avoiding power struggles, impasses, and standoffs in counseling.

Remember that in solution-focused counseling, clients' oppositions to change are conceptualized as cooperating rather than as resistance (de Shazer, 1984; Guterman, 1996a). Hence, if a client does not follow the counselor's suggestions, this is not deemed as uncooperative behavior. Instead, it is helpful information that serves to educate the counselor about how to best help the client. Many times clients are labeled as *resistant* or *in denial* simply because the counselor is not clear about the client's goals (Berg & Miller, 1992). If we look to the client for the goal rather than imposing our own notion of what the goal should be, we can often foster a more collaborative relationship. This is a particularly fitting stance to take for substance abuse because it has been suggested that enhancing cooperation between the client and counselor increases treatment compliance (Berg & Miller, 1992; de Shazer, 1984; Guterman, 1994, 1996a).

Some solution-focused writers (Berg, 1989; de Shazer, 1988) have described three types of clients: customer, complainant, and visitor. This tripartite categorization offers valuable insights for counselors in terms of understanding how to enhance cooperation during the change process when dealing with substance problems. Understanding these categories is critical when assessing who you are working with lest you create an uncooperative relationship and label your client as resistant or in denial.

The *customer* is the ideal client. They are able and willing to reach a consensus with the counselor regarding the problem and goal. The client ordinarily recognizes that he or she plays an active role in the problem and the solution. In many cases, the client is able to identify and amplify exceptions. It is likely that these clients take responsibility for their problems and are motivated to change. This is the easiest type of client to establish and maintain a cooperative working relationship with in counseling. Berg and Miller (1992) have also suggested that clinicians consider a variation of this type of client, the *hidden customer*:

> The idea of the "hidden customer" is that while clients may not initially be customers for dealing with the problem for which they were referred (e.g., alcohol), they may be customers for dealing with something else. The therapeutic rationale is that cooperation with the client's view of the problem and/or what he [or she] would like to achieve in therapy promotes cooperation, thereby facilitating progress toward treatment goals. (p. 29)

A second type of client is the *complainant*. The complainant is often able to reach a consensus with the counselor regarding the problem and goal, but he or she is usually unable to develop a solution. This type of client is also often unable to identify the concrete actions needed to solve the problem. In addition, the client might not see him- or herself as the one who needs to change and, instead, might think that someone else needs to change. In such cases, it is best for the counselor to explore the problem and goal with the client in hopes of helping him or her attain a new perspective. Sometimes this approach leads to the client changing his or her view of the problem.

The third type of client is the *visitor*. The visitor is not able to reach a consensus with the counselor regarding what the problem or goal is. The client might state that there is no problem at all, or the client might state that someone else has the problem. In such cases, the counselor should agree with the client and ask if the client wishes to work on some other problem or issue. Working on a different problem or issue might result in the client experiencing some form of treatment success which, in turn, can enhance compliance in the sessions. Sometimes this approach leads to the client changing his or her view of the problem.

TREATMENT STRATEGIES FOR SUBSTANCE PROBLEMS

A Multimodal Approach

Similar to the strategic approach to eclecticism used within my model, I find myself increasingly adopting a multimodal perspective in solution-focused counseling, especially with clients who have substance problems. Although I do not always follow as comprehensive a system as Lazarus's (1997) multimodal model, I do encourage counselors to assess clients' needs across various dimensions, including the biological, social, psychological, and spiritual. Perhaps solution-focused counseling, and all forms of counseling for that matter, are best understood as an adjunct to the larger treatment picture for substance problems because of the important role that support plays during the recovery process.

As with all cases, I do not see solution-focused counseling as *the* solution to clients' problems but, rather, as only one way to help clients find direction. This holds true when applying solution-focused counseling to substance problems.

Because there are so many resources available to assist clients during the recovery process, solution-focused counseling is to be considered as only one of a number of treatment choices. In some cases, the main purpose in solution-focused counseling is to connect or reconnect clients to community resources where they can go on to help themselves. I see value in any treatment that works. I would never advocate against a treatment model because its philosophy runs counter to my own unless, of course, I saw that it did harm to clients. If clients derive benefit from something, then I consider it to be worthwhile. If my client went to an AA meeting, an NA meeting, or a communist meeting, and it helped them, then I would consider this to be an exception.

For some clients, an intensive outpatient program is helpful. For others, a residential treatment program is what is needed for a time. The only warning I have about residential treatment programs is that they do not allow one to easily practice in vivo the insights and skills obtained from treatment. But for some clients, especially those who have repeatedly failed outpatient treatment and for those who do not have adequate support, residential treatment might be an appropriate option.

I also assess whether clients with substance problems might benefit from referrals for medication evaluations. An increasing literature has addressed the role of counseling in a society that endorses the widespread use of psychotropic medication (cf. Gladding, 2004; Glasser, 2004a, 2004b; Guterman, 2005; Pope, 2004). Compelling arguments have been made in brain science to support the view that abnormal gene expression and brain abnormalities are causally related to psychological symptoms, including addiction. To date, however, these findings have not been confirmed or refuted. Nevertheless, psychotropic medications seem to help millions of people, including those with substance problems. For example, sometimes a major depressive disorder or a sleep disorder emerges shortly after a client has remained abstinent from substances for an extended period of time. Not treating these conditions creates a risk for relapse. I recognize that there are risks and benefits to medication, and I acknowledge that medication is sometimes prescribed too frequently. But I also see medication as a pragmatic intervention for many clients with substance problems.

Replacing Substance Use Behavior

The mind cannot imagine not doing something. For example, the mind cannot comprehend "not drinking." It is crucial, then, to formulate goals in terms of the increase of something, or the addition or something, rather than the absence of something (Berg & Miller, 1992; Guterman, 1996a; Walter & Peller, 1993). Berg and Miller (1992) have suggested that "goals must be stated in positive, proactive language about what the client *will* do instead of what [he or] she will *not* do" (p. 38). So instead of setting the goal, "I will not use drugs," the client might be encouraged to set the goal, "I will attend an NA meeting if I get the urge to use drugs." Clients can be encouraged to list various potential substitutes for their substance behaviors, and these will take

Mastering the Art of Solution-Focused Counseling

the form of potential exceptions. Clients can also be asked to identify past behaviors that represent positive substitutions for their substance behaviors and these represent exceptions. Each of these—the potential exceptions and the exceptions—can then be amplified.

Learning From Relapses

An increasing literature has addressed the importance of developing relapse prevention strategies for substance problems (e.g., Marlatt & Donovan, 2005; Marlatt & Gordon, 1985). It has been suggested that people experience relapse largely because they lack adequate coping skills to deal with stressful situations, which, in turn, makes them more prone to using substances again (Marlatt & Gordon, 1985). Accordingly, relapse prevention is aimed at helping clients to identify stressful situations and to develop and practice coping skills for dealing with these situations. This strategy can be applied to a solution-focused approach to substance treatment as well. Consider the case previously described in which the client relapsed on cocaine. In that case, the counselor helped the client identify a coping method that had been used in the past to stay off of cocaine, namely, staying busy through family and household activities. The client can use this strategy as a relapse prevention strategy in the future if he gets an urge to use cocaine.

In many cases, it is helpful for clients to keep a detailed log that lists stressful events, the coping methods they employed in response to the events, and the effects of their coping methods. The log can be reviewed in counseling sessions, and clients can be helped to evaluate the effective coping methods. The log can, in turn, contribute to the client building up an armamentarium of effective coping skills as a strategy for relapse prevention.

A MANDATED CLIENT

The following case describes my work with James, a 27-year-old African American married man who was mandated to counseling by his supervisor at work after a random urine test detected marijuana. James was an assistant manager at a retail store. His employer had a drug-free workplace policy. Accordingly, James was required to participate in treatment or face termination. During the first session, James described himself as a hard worker. He stated that he had been employed as an assistant manager with the company for 3 years. He had been married for 2 years, and he had just learned that his wife became pregnant 2 months ago. According to James, last week he was asked to provide a urine sample at work and it came back positive for marijuana. But James denied having a problem with marijuana or any other substances.

> *Client:* Ah, I can't believe this happened.
> *Counselor:* Well, tell me your understanding of what happened.
> *Client:* Ah, I went into work and dropped my urine and it came back positive for weed. And here I am. But the thing is, I only smoke weed occasionally. Like once a week or less even.

Counselor: Mm hm.

Client: So they got me at a bad time.

Counselor: Okay.

Client: But I heard weed stays in your system for 30 days, so I guess I've always been vulnerable.

Counselor: Right.

Counselor: So what do *you* want to work on? Given that we have to be here.

Client: Well, I'm not an addict or anything. But I'm in big trouble now. I'm in danger of losing my job. I have to follow through with this.

Counselor: Is there anything else you want to work on?

Client: I can't have any more dirty urine or I am fired. But that's no problem. I can give it up. I haven't smoked weed since the last time. But like I said, it stays in the body for 30 days and I told my boss that. So if they ask me to give urine in the next 2 weeks, it might come back positive. But they can take my urine any time after that and I swear there will be nothing in it.

Counselor: Okay. That sounds reasonable. So you want to come to counseling to satisfy your employer's mandate. Fine.

Client: Yes.

Counselor: And you also want to continue to stay off of the weed?

Client: Yeah. I don't need it.

At this early stage, I attempted to assess the client's understanding of the problem. This was complicated by the referring person—the client's supervisor—who mandated counseling on the basis of a drug test. Nevertheless, I looked to the client for an understanding of the problem. Recalling the tripartite categorization of clients discussed earlier in this chapter, I considered what type of client James might be. Was James a customer? Was he a complainant? A visitor? Assessing this was critical in order to avoid creating resistance and, instead, establishing a cooperative client–counselor relationship from the outset.

James fit the category of hidden customer. James denied having a problem with marijuana, stating, "I only smoke weed occasionally. Like once a week or less even . . . . I'm not an addict or anything." And his goal was to attend counseling and stay clean only in order to fulfill his employer's mandate and keep his job. Some counselors might not consider this to be the "right" or "correct" goal and, instead, a reflection that James was in denial of the severity of his substance problem. I cannot say for sure whether or not James was being truthful with me, let alone himself, about the extent of his marijuana use. I am a counselor, not a detective. What I did know, however, was that James was willing to work on something. So I decided to work with James on his goal.

Working on the client's goal in this case contributed to establishing a trusting counseling relationship. It has been suggested that "because of past experiences with racism and prejudice, [African American] . . . clients are often distrustful of White counselors" (Sue & Sue, 1990, p. 220). Accordingly, it is

Mastering the Art of Solution-Focused Counseling

important to identify the expectations of African American clients—and all clients, for that matter—at the outset of treatment, including their understanding of the counseling process, their view of the history and cause of the presenting problem, issues pertaining to the limitations of confidentiality, and how long treatment shall last. Taking James's expectations into account went a long way toward creating a context conducive to positive change.

Toward the end of the first session, James inquired about the limits of confidentiality in the sessions. He had signed a release that gave me permission to disclose information to his supervisor, but I informed James that I would limit my disclosures to whether or not he was attending the sessions and my treatment recommendations. I also told James that he could rescind the release at any time. Clarifying the purpose and scope of the release seemed to help James feel more at ease. At the end of the first session, I complimented James for agreeing to a workable goal. I complimented him for making a commitment to stop using marijuana for the sake of his job and agreed to work with him in counseling. I then suggested that between now and the next session he do two things: (a) continue to do whatever you have been doing to stay off the marijuana, and (b) think about how things will be different in your life (e.g., what you will be doing differently) when you stay off the marijuana for a longer period of time, such as a year or two. James agreed to this task, and we scheduled a follow-up session in 1 week. When James presented to the second session, he was somewhat agitated.

> *Client:* I wasn't entirely honest with you last time.
> *Counselor:* Okay.
> *Client:* I've been smoking weed daily ever since I was about 16 years old. I didn't want to tell you that. I figured it was alright since I stopped for a week already. You probably think I am a liar. I *am* a liar.
> *Counselor:* It's okay.
> *Client:* Well, now you know.
> *Counselor:* Now I know. Fine. I appreciate you telling me the truth. I imagine it wasn't easy. So now, let me follow up with what I asked you about at the end of our last session.

In hopes of maintaining a cooperative relationship, I accepted the client's having been dishonest with me during the first session and reinforced his leveling with me during the second session. I created a context in which it is acceptable to lie and then to tell the truth about having lied. I forgave him. By shifting to a discussion about the task that was given at the end of the first session, I attempted to show the client that we could move forward.

> *Client:* I don't remember the task.
> *Counselor:* You don't remember?
> *Client:* Not really.

It is not uncommon for clients to forget about tasks that counselors give them in prior sessions. For this reason, it is a good idea to write down any agreed-upon task as a reminder for the client. In this instance, I did not write the task down for the client. Although the client did not remember the task, I maintained a cooperative relationship by enacting the task in the session.

> *Counselor:* That's okay. Let's think about it now. Can I remind you of what we discussed?
>
> *Client:* Sure.
>
> *Counselor:* At the end of the last session, I suggested that you do two things. First, I asked you to continue doing the things you've been doing so far to stay clean. The second thing I suggested was for you just to think about what you will do to stay off weed.
>
> *Client:* Oh, yeah.
>
> *Counselor:* You remember?
>
> *Client:* Kind of. I kind of did that already.
>
> *Counselor:* So tell me, what have you done to stay off weed? Have you still not used since our last session?
>
> *Client:* Yep. I can't or I am screwed. They'll test me anytime without warning.
>
> *Counselor:* Okay, so what have you done to stay off of it? I imagine it has taken some doing, especially since you now tell me that this has been a habit you've had for years, since you were 16 years old.

When James was given task (a), "continue to do whatever you have been doing to stay off the marijuana," the purpose was to build on existing exceptions. In the second session, James was being asked to do the same thing (i.e., identify prior exceptions).

> *Client:* Mostly, I tell myself that if I use, I lose.
>
> *Counselor:* That's true. That's very motivating for you, then?
>
> *Client:* Yes.
>
> *Counselor:* Tell me about your motivation.
>
> *Client:* It's my life. My wife's pregnant now. I can lose my job.
>
> *Counselor:* So you think about the disadvantages of using, getting caught, and the consequences it can bring.
>
> *Client:* That's right.
>
> *Counselor:* Okay. Now what else have you done to not use? For example, if you get the urge to use, what have you done instead?
>
> *Client:* Ah, lots of things.
>
> *Counselor:* What sort of things?
>
> *Client:* Well, I decided to get into something heavily, like how I was into weed.
>
> *Counselor:* Tell me about that.
>
> *Client:* I started body building. There is a gym in my apartment, so I go there sometimes.
>
> *Counselor:* You didn't go there before?
>
> *Client:* Rarely. Now I go like three times a week. I am building up my pecs and my wife sees a difference.

Mastering the Art of Solution-Focused Counseling

Counselor: So, how is that good for you?

Client: Well, it keeps me busy and I kind of get high off it. It's like a psychological high.

In this excerpt, the client stated, "If I use, I lose." I reframed this statement in terms of James's motivation to keep his job and maintain his life with his wife who is now pregnant. I then inquired about additional exceptions by asking, "If you get the urge to use, what have you done instead?" This question is aimed at replacing substance use with more adaptive behaviors. James identified body building as a replacement behavior. This exception was promptly amplified by asking James, "So how is that good for you?"

Later in the second session, I recalled task (b) by asking James to think about how things will be different in his life when he is able to stay off marijuana for an extended period of time. James stated that he would save a lot of money by not buying marijuana, he would be involved in a number of self-improvement activities (such as exercise and body building), and his head would be a lot clearer. He also acknowledged that he would be providing a better life for his family if he wasn't using marijuana.

James was mandated to attend a minimum of six counseling sessions. By the fourth session, James expressed a realization that marijuana had been a significant problem in his life and that he really was better off without it. He stated that it was difficult at times to keep his mind off of his urges to use marijuana, but it was becoming easier. This case reinforced my view that working on the client's goals can sometimes lead to the client changing his or her view about the problem. After our sixth session, I informed James that he was no longer required to continue counseling as he had made sufficient progress. But James stated that he wanted to continue treatment to ensure that he maintained his gains and, also, to work on other issues in his life. James was no longer a mandated client.

CONCLUDING REMARKS

Substance abuse is a serious problem for people and society, and it has become increasingly important for counselors to develop effective treatment approaches for this condition. In this chapter, solution-focused applications to substance problems have been described. Solution-focused counseling offers a basis from which to reconceptualize resistance and enhance cooperation during the change process. In addition, the model is compatible with a multimodal approach that includes other treatments during the recovery process. It is suggested that future research assess outcome effectiveness related to solution-focused applications to substance problems.

CHAPTER 9

Grief, Suicide, Trichotillomania, and Other Problems

A flexible clinical approach speaks to Paul's (1967) cogent point that counseling is to be evaluated in terms of how it addresses the question of "*what* treatment by *whom*, is most effective for *this* individual, under what set of circumstances" (p. 117). No model is a panacea, including solution-focused counseling. But given solution-focused counseling's ability to incorporate virtually any content within its change process, including formal content and techniques from other counseling theories, it is to be considered a comprehensive clinical system capable of addressing a wide breadth and scope of problems and client populations. In this chapter, I describe the application of solution-focused counseling to various clinical problems and client populations.

GRIEF

The Problem

In recent years, an increasing literature has set forth solution-focused applications to grief and bereavement (Butler & Powers, 1996; Davy, 1999; Gray, Zide, & Wilker, 2000). I have been asked by workshop attendees whether solution-focused counseling is a fitting model for clients who are experiencing grief. Some counselors and students express concern that the model is "too positive" for such tragic problems. I quickly suggest, however, that solution-focused counseling works quite well in such cases *if* it is used appropriately.

The key to using solution-focused counseling for the problem of grief is to recognize that success lies in developing a supportive relationship with the client. First and foremost, it is necessary to employ fundamental counseling skills, including listening, reflecting, and empathy. The basics of solution-focused counseling also need to be followed, such as joining, respecting the client's worldview, and working on the client's chosen problems and goals. In particular, there are two principles I keep in mind when doing solution-focused grief counseling: *acknowledgment* and a *future-orientation*.

The first principle—acknowledgment—has been described by Butler and Powers (1996):

> *Acknowledgment* is fundamental. It is what we call "being with the client." In a sense, it is as if we place ourselves in the same location or position as the client in his or her process of dealing with the problem. It is similar to the basic Rogerian attitude of reflecting the client's feelings, accepting his or her position, and trusting his or her capacity for self-direction (Rogers, 1951). The practical expressions of this idea are the basic therapeutic techniques of listening, mirroring, paraphrasing/reflecting, summarizing, and conveying empathy through facial expressions, tone of voice, and so on. (p. 229)

In keeping with a postmodern orientation, there is no one right or correct way to grieve. Accordingly, acknowledgment also involves accepting the client's unique way of coping with his or her loss. Sometimes clients put added pressure on themselves by insisting that they are not grieving properly. For example, after reading Elizabeth Kubler-Ross's (1969) book, *On Death and Dying*, a client felt that she was not proceeding through the stages of grief in a proper fashion. In other cases, one family member might express concern or even blame another for the way he or she is dealing with the loss. There is a wide range of normality with regard to grief processes. In fact, there is no right way to grieve. Everyone grieves in their own unique way. Acknowledgment involves helping clients accept their own and others' unique styles of grieving.

The second principle I follow is a future orientation, which involves helping clients to focus on goals. It involves directing clients to focus on their strengths, resources, and effective problem-solving skills. This is when the counselor dares to be solution-focused despite the loss that the client has suffered. Given the loss involved in grief and bereavement cases, the counselor may choose to go slow. The counselor should be particularly mindful of the importance of timing and pacing. Perhaps the techniques and tasks will be used differently than in other cases. The counselor might adopt a more gradual, tentative approach. In some cases, a slower approach might not be necessary or appropriate. Regardless of the timing involved, solution-focused techniques can be used in a manner that retains and, moreover, enhances the principle of acknowledgment during grief and bereavement counseling. The case that follows describes the use of solution-focused counseling in grief work.

Case Example

A 45-year-old woman came to counseling following the death of her mother. The client had been diagnosed with a major depressive disorder prior to her mother's death. Since her mother died 4 months ago, she had become even more depressed and sought counseling to cope with her loss and deal with the exacerbation of the depression. During the first session, the counselor encouraged the client to express her feelings of grief. The counselor attempted to be empathic and normalized the client's feelings as part of the grief process. Rather than give the client a solution-focused task at the end of the first session, the counselor complimented the client for seeking help and suggested that a second appointment be scheduled in 1 week.

During the second session, the client continued to express her feelings of grief. The counselor then attempted to help the client *map the influences of the problem* (see chapter 6). I have found this to be a useful technique in cases of loss because it addresses the two principles of solution-focused grief counseling: acknowledgment and a future orientation. First, the counselor asks the client to identify ways in which the loss has affected various aspects of the client's life. Doing so helps the counselor acknowledge the client's problem. Second, the influences serve as a basis from which to later identify exceptions. After the client has identified various influences of the problem, the counselor can go back to these influences and inquire about exceptions.

In this case, the counselor asked the client how the loss of her mother had affected her life across various dimensions, including work and her social life. The client reported that she was often unable to concentrate at work. She stated that she no longer engaged in hobbies such as singing in her church choir. She also stated that she seldom socialized with her two best friends. Again, the counselor did not give the client a task at the end of the second session. The counselor and client agreed to meet in 1 week for another session. The following excerpt illustrates the application of a future orientation that was adopted by the counselor at the start of the third session:

> *Counselor:* What's better?
> *Client:* I've been doing some more things.
> *Counselor:* You have?
> *Client:* Yes.
> *Counselor:* What have you been doing?
> *Client:* I've been trying to get more involved.
> *Counselor:* More involved?
> *Client:* That talk we had last time. I've given up on everything. So I decided to get back to doing some things.
> *Counselor:* Excellent. What things have you done?
> *Client:* I called my friend and we went out. That's about it.
> *Counselor:* That's great.
> *Client:* Yeah.
> *Counselor:* Now tell me something . . .
> *Client:* Sure.
> *Counselor:* How did you get yourself to call her up? I ask this because you haven't done it all this time and now suddenly you did it.

Client: I don't know, um, I just thought I need to do this.
Counselor: That's great. That's great.

The counselor's question "What's better?" was interventive insofar as it created the expectancy that indeed there was improvement since the previous session. When the client replied, "I've been doing some more things," the counselor followed up with a line of questioning to determine whether there were exceptions. It turned out that an exception was derived from one of the influences of the problem that had been mapped during the previous session, namely, going out with her friend. The counselor then attempted to amplify this exception by asking, "How did you get yourself to call her up?" The rest of the session involved the counselor helping the client to identify and amplify various exceptions to the problem of depression and grief. At the end of the third session, the counselor gave the client the task to observe for times when she was able to make exceptions happen. The counselor and client continued to meet on a regular basis. Although the sessions took on more of a solution focus, the client occasionally slipped back to episodes of profound grief. After 2 months of counseling, however, the client reported that she was socializing more, that she had resumed participating in her church choir, and that she was able to function better at work. Eventually, it was agreed that counseling was no longer needed.

This case illustrates the application of solution-focused counseling to the problem of grief. The counselor followed the principle of acknowledgment during the early stage of treatment by encouraging the client to express her feelings in a supportive and caring environment. As counseling progressed, the counselor shifted to a future orientation by using solution-focused techniques. In the process, the counselor emphasized the client's existing resources and problem-solving abilities to develop a solution.

SUICIDE

The Problem

Perhaps no event is feared more in the professional life of a counselor than the prospect of a client completing suicide. The suicide of a client brings with it the potential for a lawsuit as well as added psychological stress such as the counselor feeling as if he or she could have or should have done more. Although suicide remains a relatively rare event, epidemiological studies have shown that up to 5% of the population have made a suicide attempt and up to 20% have experienced suicidal ideation at some time in their lives (Cox, Enns, & Clara, 2004). It has also been noted that over 50% of people who attempt suicide are already receiving some form of mental health services (Hawkes, Marsh, & Wilgosh, 1998). Accordingly, mental health professionals, including counselors, have a responsibility to develop effective assessment skills and interventions aimed at reducing risk and potential harm of clients.

In recent years, a number of theorists and practitioners have suggested that solution-focused models are effective for dealing with suicidal clients (Hawkes

Mastering the Art of Solution-Focused Counseling

et al., 1998; Sharry, Darmody, & Madden, 2002; Softas-Nall & Francis, 1998a, 1998b). Sharry et al. (2002) have pointed out that some counselors might express caution about using a solution-focused approach with suicidal clients "given its lack of emphasis on risk assessment." (p. 385). I agree that there is a paucity of writing in the solution-focused literature on risk assessment. This is unfortunate because such an omission might lead some counselors to generalize that solution-focused models do not carefully assess suicide risk and take steps to ensure the safety of clients when necessary.

My solution-focused counseling approach involves conducting a formal intake, including a thorough mental status examination. This allows me to assess suicidal ideation, plan, means, intent, family history, and so forth. If the client is an imminent danger to him- or herself, then I am required to direct him or her to a safe environment, such as a hospital. If they are unwilling to go to a hospital, then I am required by law to initiate involuntary placement on their behalf. Assuming clients are immediately safe, I have found solution-focused counseling to be an effective model from which to help them use their existing problem-solving skills to cope with suicidal thoughts and focus on the future. The following case example describes the use of solution-focused counseling with a client with a history of chronic suicidal thoughts and multiple suicide attempts.

Case Example

A 26-year-old single female named Lisa came to counseling after being released from a psychiatric hospital following a suicide attempt. The client had made superficial cuts to her wrist following an argument with her boyfriend. Her boyfriend was with her at home when she cut her wrist. He called the police, and she was taken to the hospital. Lisa reported a history of multiple suicide attempts and psychiatric hospitalizations since age 15. She reported that she had been given a diagnosis of borderline personality disorder by numerous mental health professionals. During the first session, the counselor conducted a thorough risk assessment and determined that although the client had death wishes at the present time, she denied suicidal ideation, plan, or intent and was not an imminent danger to herself. The client and counselor discussed the client's long history of suicidal thoughts and suicide attempts. The client reported that she often attempted suicide or experienced thoughts of suicide whenever she was under stress.

> *Counselor:* Tell me about a time when you felt under stress and thought about suicide, but you didn't do it.
> *Client:* I didn't do it?
> *Counselor:* Right. You *didn't* do it.
> *Client:* Well, there have been a lot of times like that.
> *Counselor:* Okay.
> *Client:* Sometimes I think of doing it and I don't because I think of my mother.

Counselor: What about her?

Client: I think that I don't want to put her through that. She has enough problems. She doesn't need to have her daughter kill herself.

Counselor: Right.

Client: I also think of another thing. I sometimes think that they're only going to put me in the hospital for a day or two and that's not going to do me any good. It's a hassle. That place does me no good ever. So why bother?

Counselor: I see. So you think that it's not worth it? Is that it?

Client: Yeah. I might as well forget it.

Counselor: Forget it?

Client: Yeah. Forget about cutting or taking pills.

Counselor: And then what happens? After you decide to not do it, to not take the pills?

Client: It is okay. I am okay. It passes.

Counselor: It passes?

Client: Yeah.

Counselor: It passes.

Client: Yeah, it passes. For a while. Until next time.

This excerpt illustrates the counselor's attempt at using solution-focused techniques to identify exceptions to the client's problem of suicidal thoughts. In this excerpt, two exceptions were identified. First, the client stated, "Sometimes I think of doing it and I don't because I think of my mother." Second, the client convinced herself that it is not worth cutting or taking pills because it is a hassle to go to the hospital. The counselor worked with this client for the next year with mixed results. The client continued to report suicidal thoughts off and on. At some point in treatment, the counselor helped the client shift her attention to the future by asking questions along the lines of "How will things in your life be different when you are able to consistently resist acting on the suicidal thoughts?" The client was hospitalized twice for suicide attempts during the time when she was in treatment with the counselor. Eventually, the client moved out of state with her mother and therefore discontinued treatment with the counselor.

It is reaffirmed that solution-focused counseling is a potentially effective approach to treat clients who are suicidal. Assuming that a thorough risk assessment has been done, the solution-focused process of helping clients to identify and amplify exceptions to cope with suicidal thoughts can be applied. This case illustrated the application of solution-focused counseling to a client who had been diagnosed with borderline personality disorder in which chronic suicidal ideation and multiple suicide attempts are a classic symptom. It is not surprising, then, that this client experienced limited success in solution-focused counseling. Nevertheless, the client was hospitalized only twice during the year when she was receiving solution-focused counseling, which was a marked improvement from her baseline.

Mastering the Art of Solution-Focused Counseling

TRICHOTILLOMANIA

The Problem

According to the *DSM–IV–TR*, trichotillomania is an impulse control disorder involving the recurrent pulling out of one's hair sometimes resulting in noticeable hair loss (APA, 2000). Clients often experience an increase in tension or anxiety immediately before pulling out their hair or if they attempt to resist pulling out their hair. Conversely, clients often report relief, pleasure, or gratification after pulling out their hair. In order for the *DSM–IV–TR* criteria to be met for trichotillomania, the client must experience clinically significant distress about the hair pulling or impairment in social, occupational, or other important areas of functioning as a result of the behavior (APA, 2000).

It has been estimated that over 2 million people in the United States meet criteria for trichotillomania (Diefenbach, Reitman, & Williamson, 2000). It has been suggested, however, that the prevalence of trichotillomania is underestimated for various reasons. The diagnosis is sometimes missed by clinicians because it is comorbid with other disorders (Mulinari-Brenner & Bergfeld, 2001). Nevertheless, trichotillomania is a relatively rare disorder. According to V. E. White, Kelly, and McCormick (2004), "many clinicians have had little or no experience working with this population . . . [and] counselors have an obligation to become educated about the assessment, diagnosis, and treatment of trichotillomania" (p. 185). The onset of trichotillomania usually occurs during late childhood and can become a chronic condition if it goes untreated (Stein, Christenson, & Hollander, 1999; V. E. White et al., 2004). Several prominent theories regarding the etiology of this disorder have been formulated, including psychodynamic (Diefenbach et al., 2000), behavioral (Michael, 2004), and biological (Palmer, Yates, & Trotter, 1999). A review of the literature reveals that medication, behavior therapy, cognitive therapy, and hypnotherapy are potentially effective treatments for trichotillomania. Following is a case example that illustrates the application of solution-focused counseling to the problem of trichotillomania. The positive results of this case suggest that this model holds promise as an effective intervention for this condition.

Case Example

A 9-year-old girl named Bailey was referred to counseling by her pediatrician for recurrent hair pulling. Bailey came to the first session accompanied by her mother, Patty. Patty was divorced from Bailey's father 6 years ago. Bailey was an only child. In the first session, a thorough assessment was conducted, and it was determined that Bailey did not have a comorbid mental disorder. According to the mother, Bailey started pulling her hair out 2 years ago, and the frequency had increased to one or two episodes daily. The mother described the hair pulling episodes as follows. Bailey would pull out a clump of her hair and then wrap it around her index finger on her left hand. Bailey would then suck her thumb from the same hand while placing her index finger with the hair wrapped around it immediately under her nose. The mother felt that Bailey sucked her thumb as a way to cope with anxiety and stress. The mother also noted that Bailey always seemed to be comforted after this process, which ended in her sucking her thumb with the hair under her nose. Bailey had a few noticeable bald spots as a result of her hair pulling. Otherwise, she appeared normal in every other respect.

During the first session, I questioned Patty and Bailey in detail about the hair pulling process. And it seemed as if I was going nowhere until I asked the mother a simple question that changed the course of counseling: "What have you tried to deal with this problem that *has* worked?" The mother smiled and answered my question without hesitation. "One thing has seemed to work," Patty replied quickly. Patty went on to describe a most creative solution. It seemed that Bailey also found comfort in using her mother's hair while sucking her thumb. The mother had observed that on some occasions while at home, Bailey would snuggle up to her, wrap her index finger around her mother's long hair, and then suck her thumb from the same hand. Patty initially discouraged this behavior. But after thinking about it, she reconsidered because it seemed like a better alternative to Bailey pulling out her own hair. Six months ago, Patty decided to cut off locks of her own hair and give them to Bailey to take to school and elsewhere. The mother instructed Bailey to use her mother's hair rather than pull out her own if she had the desire to suck her thumb. Unfortunately, Bailey seldom followed through. Patty explained that at school Bailey would either lose her mother's locks or forget to pull out the locks and resort to pulling out her own hair.

Toward the end of the first session, I complimented Patty for coming up with such a creative solution to such a difficult problem. I suggested that she seemed to be on the right track, but a stronger and more consistent effort was needed. I agreed that using the mother's hair was an acceptable alternative to Bailey pulling out her own hair. Both Patty and Bailey agreed. I also agreed that it was a good idea to prepare locks of the mother's hair for Bailey to carry with her at all times. But I raised the question as to how Bailey would remember to pull out the locks when it was time to suck her thumb. I asked Patty and Bailey if they had any idea of how Bailey could remember to pull out her mother's locks. Bailey said that she had an idea. She said, "Just like I pull out *my* hair, I can remember the words *pull out*, but I'll pull out my mother's hair." Patty and I told Bailey that this was a great way to remember. I suggested, however, that more ways to remember were needed. I recommended that because the mother's locks were tied with string, Bailey could tie a string around her index finger, the location where she placed the hair, and this would serve as a reminder to pull out her mother's hair. Both agreed that this would help. I suggested yet another way to remember. Bailey's teacher could be told about the plan so that she could provide reminders if needed. Both also agreed to this strategy. A follow-up session was scheduled in 1 week.

In the second session, the mother reported that she and Bailey had followed the plan. According to the mother, Bailey had pulled out her own hair on only two occasions during the past week, which was a marked reduction from the previous one to two episodes daily. After 3 weeks of counseling, the hair pulling ceased completely.

An argument could be made that the client in this case might not have met the full *DSM–IV–TR* criteria for trichotillomania. An increasing literature has suggested that for some clients hair pulling is a relatively benign habit similar to thumb sucking (Byrd, Richards, & Hove, 2002; Friman, 1992). Nevertheless, this case illustrates how a solution-focused intervention served to interrupt a behavioral pattern that alarmed the client's pediatrician and mother. Solution-focused counseling provided a timely and minimalist intervention that avoided what otherwise might have been a more intrusive treatment episode for the client. As for the client's thumb sucking, some might argue that this problem was left unresolved. Most children stop sucking their thumb or other fingers around the age of 4 or 5 (Byrd et al., 2002). After that age, thumb sucking can cause problems with the teeth or jaw line (Friman, 1992). Although it would have been preferable to address the client's thumb sucking behavior given that she was 9 years old, I made the clinical judgment to bypass this problem. On the basis of the particulars in this case, the risks involved seemed too great to take the thumb sucking away from the client. The client's hair pulling was of most concern to those persons involved, including me. My hope was that the client would naturally outgrow her thumb-sucking habit.

GENERALIZED ANXIETY DISORDER

The Problem

According to the *DSM–IV–TR*, "the essential feature of generalized anxiety disorder is excessive anxiety and worry (apprehensive expectation), occurring more days than not for a period of at least 6 months, about a number of events or activities" (APA, 2000, p. 472). It has been estimated that approximately 5% of the world population suffer from generalized anxiety disorder (Riskind, 2005). Yet generalized anxiety disorder is only one of a number of anxiety disorders listed in the *DSM*. Other anxiety disorders listed in the *DSM* include, but are not limited to, panic disorder, agoraphobia, specific phobia, social phobia, obsessive–compulsive disorder, posttraumatic stress disorder, and acute stress disorder. Although these disorders can be distinguished from one another in terms of their respective diagnostic criteria, they are similar insofar as they each include prominent symptoms of anxiety. The following case example illustrates the application of solution-focused counseling to generalized anxiety disorder. The following case also illustrates how solution-focused counseling can be used for other anxiety disorders as well.

Case Example

A 31-year-old single male named George came to counseling with complaints of sweating palms, heart palpitations, and dizziness for the past year. George had consulted with his primary care physician due to these symptoms and was medically cleared. He was then referred to counseling by his primary care physician due to an anxiety problem. During the first session, George reported that he had many worries. He frequently worried about finances and losing his job. He also frequently worried about the health of his parents. George stated that although he recognized that his worries were unrealistic, he could not stop worrying.

During the first session, the counselor was unsuccessful at identifying exceptions to the problem of worrying. Accordingly, a variation of the miracle question was posed to the client. The client was asked, "Imagine that your worst fear is realized and that you are coping effectively. What will you be doing?" The rationale for this question is to focus the client's attention on coping effectively in the worst scenario. It is assumed that worry largely consists of anticipatory fear and catastrophizing; if clients envision themselves coping effectively in the feared situation, then worry will dissipate (Rygh & Sanderson, 2004).

> *Client:* Actually, I have thought about that already.
>
> *Counselor:* You've already imagined one of these bad things happening *and* coping effectively with it?
>
> *Client:* Maybe not coping well. But I've thought about what it would be like if it happened.
>
> *Counselor:* Okay, but I am asking you to think about what you will be doing when you are coping well.
>
> *Client:* Oh.
>
> *Counselor:* Right. So would you think about that now? What will you be doing if you were, say, sad about losing your job, but not totally destroyed?
>
> *Client:* I might think that it's not the end of the world.
>
> *Counselor:* Yes, it's not the end of the world.
>
> *Client:* Or I can get another job.
>
> *Counselor:* Yes. You will get another job.
>
> *Client:* So there is no use in worrying.
>
> *Counselor:* Exactly.

During the first session, the revised miracle question was systematically applied to each of the client's prominent worries, and the client was able to picture himself coping satisfactorily in each of these scenarios. Although the client reported generalized anxiety in addition to worry about specific situations, the main focus of the first session was on his worry. At the end of the first session, a version of Task 3 (see chapter 5) was given to the client. The client was told and asked the following:

> Between now and the next session, I would like you to practice the exercise we did in the session today. Imagine that your worst fear is realized (e.g., you lose your job, you go bankrupt, your parents become ill or even die) *and* you are coping effectively. So I want you to imagine precisely what you will be doing to cope effectively in each of these scenarios. The things you will be doing, such as how you will think about the situation, specific behaviors, and so forth. Then be sure to make note of these effective coping skills so that we can discuss them during the next session.

Mastering the Art of Solution-Focused Counseling

At the start of the second session, the client reported that during the past week he had practiced the task on several occasions. The client reported that in most instances he was successful at imagining himself coping effectively in the feared scenarios. He recalled that similar to the enactment of this task during the first session, the most common effective coping skill that contributed to reducing worry was a change in his thinking. More specifically, the client reported holding a less catastrophic view of the feared situations. The client stated that he felt as if he had already begun to internalize a more realistic perspective about these feared situations. As a result, he was experiencing a significant reduction in his generalized anxiety. At the end of the second session, the counselor suggested that the client apply his new perspective whenever he found himself worrying. In addition, the client was asked to use the scaling technique to assess and, also, identify and amplify exceptions in relation to his generalized anxiety.

During the third session, the client reported that he was virtually free of worry. He attributed his progress to adopting a less catastrophic view of the situations that he had previously feared. The scaling technique revealed numerous effective coping skills (exceptions) for the client's generalized anxiety. The scales obtained in the third session served as the client's baseline, which were then compared with the scales derived later in treatment. This comparison showed marked improvement in the client's generalized anxiety. After 10 sessions, the client reported that he seldom experienced sweating palms, heart palpitations, or dizziness. The counselor and client agreed that further counseling was no longer required.

MORBID JEALOUSY

The Problem

It is difficult to imagine a human relationship that has not been touched at some time to some degree by jealousy. In its mildest form, jealousy can be understood as a sign of love, caring, and devotion. When jealousy is out of control, however, it can lead to obsessiveness and violence. In recent years, a consensus has been reached regarding the meaning of the term *morbid jealousy* (e.g., Bishay, Tarrier, & Dolan, 1996; Dolan & Bishay, 1996; Keenan & Farrell, 2000; Tarrier, Beckett, & Harwood, 1990). According to Bishay et al. (1996), morbid jealousy is defined as excessive and irrational preoccupation with a partner's fidelity (or suspicion of infidelity) when there is no objective foundation. Dolan and Bishay (1996) have pointed out that these preoccupations are often triggered by memories, including mental images, of a partner's past or present romantic and sexual relationships. According to Dolan and Bishay (1996), these memories activate negative beliefs about the self that center around unworthiness and unattractiveness (e.g., Ellis, 1996d). These beliefs predispose clients to misinterpret their partners' behaviors, and these misinterpretations result in jealous reactions.

Various treatment approaches have been applied to morbid jealousy, including cognitive–behavioral (Bishay et al., 1996), couples counseling (de Silva,

2004), medication (Stein, Hollander, & Josephson, 1994), and integrative models (Pines, 1992). In contrast to these treatment strategies, solution-focused counseling holds that clients with morbid jealousy have existing or potential problem-solving skills that can be used in the development of therapeutic solutions. Accordingly, solution-focused counseling is organized around looking to the client for identifying and amplifying exceptions to the problem. Following is a case example of a solution-focused application to morbid jealousy.

Case Example

A 29-year-old Cuban American man named Willy presented to counseling. Willy had been married to Elena for 1 year. This was the first marriage for both. They had dated for about 2 years prior to being married. Elena was also Cuban American. Both Willy and Elena were born in the United States. They had no children. During their courtship, Elena would frequently bring up her past boyfriends in casual conversations. Willy described himself as a jealous type, so he found it particularly difficult to deal with her frequent mentions of her past romantic relationships. When they were dating, the couple would have severe arguments whenever Elena mentioned her previous boyfriends. At one point, the couple broke up because of this problem. Eventually, Elena agreed to never talk about her past relationships again, and the subject became taboo. Soon after marrying, however, Willy began to experience intrusive thoughts about his wife's past. Although he had previously demanded that she stop talking about her past, he began to initiate the subject. Willy would drill Elena about her sexual history. He then convinced her to disclose the most intimate details about her sexual past by assuring her that having such information would help him confront his fears and overcome his jealousy.

Willy learned that Elena had intercourse with eight men prior to their marriage. Elena told Willy the names of each of these men. Willy even asked Elena to compare the size of his penis with her past sexual partners. Unfortunately, Elena complied. Willy's jealousy was fueled when Elena informed him that all of her past sexual partners were larger than he was except for two. Eventually, Elena refused to feed into Willy's jealousy and stopped answering any questions about her sexual past. Over the course of the next few months, Willy became more and more obsessed about Elena's past. Willy escalated even further after Elena informed him that she had a chance encounter with one of her ex-boyfriends at a shopping mall. After that incident, Willy frequently became suspicious that Elena might leave him for one of her ex-boyfriends. He also began a ritual of seeking constant reassurance from Elena as to whether or not she had any encounters with any of her ex-boyfriends.

When Willy came to the first counseling session, he was agitated, he was clearly in emotional pain, he was depressed, and he seemed desperate to get help. Following is an excerpt from the first counseling session.

> *Client:* I want to get to a place where I know that what she did in the past is completely unimportant.

Counselor: Okay.

Client: But I am not there now.

Counselor: Okay. Where are you now?

Client: I'm not well.

Counselor: Okay. Tell me about it.

Client: She's the girl of my dreams. You understand that?

Counselor: I'm trying.

Client: That's the first thing you need to understand. This is not just any girl. This is the one. *[Takes a photograph out of his wallet and shows it to the counselor]* You see this?

Counselor: [Looks at photograph] She's beautiful.

Client: Alright. I can't imagine her having been with any other guy. Can you understand that? But I want to get to a place where I know that it doesn't matter. Can you understand that?

Counselor: Let me see if I have this right. You want to get to a place where you can accept, basically, that she was with other guys.

Client: Right.

This excerpt illustrates the client's effort to convey his understanding of the problem. The counselor prefaced his understanding by using the hedging statement, "Let me see if I have this right." Willy then agreed with the counselor's understanding, "You want to get to a place where you can accept, basically, that she was with other guys." At this stage, the counselor also considered the degree to which masculine gender roles specific to the client's culture might or might not influence the presenting problem. Sue and Sue (1990) have noted that with regard to Latin Americans, "men are expected to be strong, dominant, and the provider for the family whereas women are expected to be nurturant, submissive to the male, and self-sacrificing" (p. 233). Traditionally, *machismo* is the term used to denote hypermasculine gender roles specific to Latin cultures. Some characteristics of machismo associated with a hypermasculine perspective are male dominance, authoritarianism, sexism, oppressive and controlling behaviors toward women, bravado, and honor (Ramirez, 1999; Torres, 1998; Torres, Solberg, & Carlstrom, 2002). In recent years, however, some researchers (e.g., Ramirez, 1999; Torres et al., 2002) have suggested that alternative, more positive conceptions of machismo are emerging in Latin cultures. These alternative characteristics include being family oriented, hard working, loving, and protective of one's family, and having an interest in the welfare of less fortunate members of society.

The counselor spent much of the first session and portions of subsequent sessions striving to understand the degree to which the client's machismo might have contributed to and maintained his morbid jealousy. It was apparent that Willy held the view that Elena's past sexual history was an insult to his masculinity. Even though he had many sexual experiences before the marriage—too numerous to count, according to Willy—even the thought of his wife having sex with another man was a personal assault on his machismo. But there also seemed to be a dissonance lurking between, on one hand, his traditional beliefs about gender roles and, on the other hand, his desire to accept the reality that his wife had a sexual past.

Willy met with the counselor on an ongoing basis for the next 3 months. During the course of treatment, the counselor followed a largely generic, rather than eclectic, approach to solution-focused counseling (see chapter 3). Gradually, the client reported a reduction in the frequency and intensity of his jealous emotions and behaviors. Following is an excerpt from a counseling session at a stage in treatment when Willy had shown marked improvement.

> *Counselor:* What is different between how you look at the past now and how you used to see it?
> *Client:* I realize now that it doesn't matter. It's like, So what!
> *Counselor:* To say "So what!" is a big change. That's a huge shift.
> *Client:* Yeah. It's not important what she did.
> *Counselor:* Right. That's a big change. The question is, How did you do that?

The counselor's question, "What is different between how you look at the past now and how you used to see it?" is designed to identify exceptions to the client's jealousy. The client responded by offering the perspective, "So what!" as a response to his wife's sexual past. The counselor then asked, "The question is, How did you do that?" This question is aimed at amplifying the exception, obtaining a thicker description of what the client has done to make the positive change, and thereby create a context from which to help the client ascribe significant meaning to the change.

> *Client:* I don't know. *[Silent for a few moments]* Maybe I thought about it and realized how silly it is. *[Silent again for a few moments]* So what! So she did it with some guys. It's not the end of the world and it really doesn't mean anything about me. So I'll forget about it. She's with me now and that's the end of it.
> *Counselor:* Well, that's . . .
> *Client: [Interrupts]* And I really have no reason to believe she's going to do anything with any guys now.
> *Counselor:* . . . a big change.

The preceding excerpt illustrates the counselor's attempt to amplify the client's exception, "So what!" to a new understanding regarding his wife's sexual past, namely, "It's not the end of the world and it really doesn't mean anything about me." It became clear that the client also experienced an exceptional shift in terms of his sense of machismo. Whereas Willy experienced a hypermasculine sense of machismo at the onset of counseling, it appeared that he was shifting to an alternative, more positive masculine gender role as a result of the progress he had made in treatment. After 6 months of counseling, the counselor and client agreed that Willy had maintained his progress and that further treatment

Mastering the Art of Solution-Focused Counseling

was no longer needed. It was agreed that Willy could resume counseling in the future if the need should arise.

Willy contacted the counselor 7 years later to resume treatment. He reported that 6 months ago, he and his wife had their first and only child, a daughter named Ines. Willy's father had died of a sudden heart attack shortly after Ines was born. Then Willy's mother died 1 month later in a car accident. Willy became very depressed soon thereafter and was resuming treatment to cope with the loss of his parents and his severe depression. During this second course of treatment, Elena filed for divorce. According to Willy, his depression had become so severe that he was hardly able to function. He would immediately climb in bed upon returning home from work and found himself becoming increasingly alienated from his wife, child, family, and friends. He had also consulted with a psychiatrist and was placed on an antidepressant. Then Willy learned that his wife was having an affair with a coworker. Willy learned of the affair shortly after being served with divorce papers. Although Willy reported experiencing a severe exacerbation of his depression (e.g., severely disorganized thinking, depersonalization) for the first 2 days after learning of the affair, these symptoms quickly remitted. Willy then reported a marked transformation for the better. Following is an excerpt from a counseling session at this stage in the treatment.

> *Client:* My worst fear was realized. It came true. And it's not the end of the world. I was right.
>
> *Counselor:* You were right?
>
> *Client:* I still can't believe it. That she went with this guy. But it's not the end of the world. And screw them. Screw them both. And when it happened, when I realized that she did that, I did a simple thing to get over it. I decided right then and there that I would withdraw my love from her. If she wants to cheat on me and not be with me and do that, then I won't love her anymore.
>
> *Counselor:* And you did that?
>
> *Client:* Yes I did. Some people might think it's impossible. And I don't care. I don't care! I know what I feel. And if she can do that to me, to our relationship, then I can withdraw my love that easily.
>
> *Counselor:* And if that works for you, then fine.

Although the counselor was initially skeptical of Willy's claim that he was able to resolve his wife's affair by "withdrawing his love," he accepted the client's statement. But it seemed that the client was able to do just that. Willy showed sudden gains (see chapter 7) in his depression. Within a month, Willy was separated from his wife and his mood was significantly improved. Within 2 months, Willy reported that he was happier than he had ever been in his life. His divorce became finalized. He began socializing with a new circle of friends. And he reported that he had finally found himself. After 3 months, Willy and the counselor agreed that further treatment was no longer necessary.

Three year later, Willy contacted the counselor again and requested to resume treatment. This time he reported that he had fallen deeply in love with another woman. Her name was Pilar, and she was also Cuban American. He was considering marrying Pilar and wanted counseling to address various premarital issues. Willy eventually married Pilar and continued to see the counselor on a sporadic basis when this book went to press. Willy, although significantly improved with regard to his tendency to become jealous, is not invulnerable to this problem in his relationship with Pilar. Nevertheless, he is much less jealous than he used to be. Additionally, he is more able to be self-effacing and not take himself too seriously. This attitude has, in turn, impacted his marital relationship and some of his other important relationships quite favorably.

CONCLUDING REMARKS

In this chapter, I have described solution-focused applications to various clinical problems and client populations. Although no one model can be all things for all people at all times, it is suggested that solution-focused counseling is a comprehensive clinical system capable of addressing a wide breadth and scope of problems (e.g., Guterman, 1996a; Guterman & Leite, in press; Guterman et al., 2005). Each case was similar insofar as the informal content was subsumed within solution-focused counseling's problem/exception ascription (i.e., formal content). This feature of solution-focused counseling, namely, the generalizability of its formal content across cases, makes the model well suited for addressing a variety of problems and clinical situations. I invite readers to consider using solution-focused counseling for a variety of problems in hopes of expanding the potential applications of this model.

CHAPTER 10
Jared's Complaint

In this chapter, a case example describing my work with one client is provided to exemplify the theory and practice of solution-focused counseling. This case describes my experiences with Jared, a White Jewish man whom I first met in 1985 when I began working as a counselor on a psychiatric unit in Fort Lauderdale, Florida. At the time, Jared was 32 years old and was given a diagnosis of schizophrenia. Jared was hospitalized on multiple occasions from 1985 to 1989 when I worked at the hospital. I never saw or heard from Jared again after I left my position there in 1989. Then, one day in 1993, he left a message at my private office.

"My doctor won't see me anymore!" Jared screamed.

"Why not?" I asked.

"I don't know. I don't know. I guess I've been calling his office too many times. He's had it with me. Can you help me? Can you refer me to another doctor!?"

From my memory, I recalled that Jared was not the easiest client to deal with. But Jared's doctor was not the most patient, either. I agreed to help Jared. I suggested a referral to Dr. Aptakar, a psychiatrist whom I worked closely with and trusted. I made the referral and thought that was the end of it. But 1 week later, Jared called me again.

"How did it go?" I asked.

"Fine," Jared said. "Dr. Aptakar will see me, but he said he wants me in counseling with you. So I have to set an appointment."

Dr. Aptakar often did that. If I referred a client to him, he would follow them if they needed medication. But he would be sure to also refer them back to me for counseling. I wasn't sure if it was appropriate for me to see Jared, though. I had questions concerning whether he was even amenable to counseling given his chronic mental illness, but I reluctantly agreed.

COUNSELING WITH JARED

Although I knew Jared from when I had worked on the psychiatric unit in the 1980s, when I met with him for our first session in 1993 he provided me with a history that I could never have imagined.

Jared was an only child. He was born in New York and raised Jewish. He moved to Florida with his parents in 1973 at the age of 20. He had his first psychotic break when he was 23 years old. Since then, he had been hospitalized on multiple occasions. Jared gave me lurid accounts of some of his psychotic episodes.

"I ate my own shit once," Jared told me.

Jared told me that his one joy in life was going to prostitutes. Other than prostitutes, he had never had a sexual relationship with a female. Dr. Aptakar thought this was an ominous sign. Jared was on disability and did not have much money. He lived in a modest apartment; his parents provided him with financial assistance when they could although they were not very well off. But whenever Jared was able to get some money together, he would treat himself to having sex with a prostitute. He did this about three or four times a year. Jared provided me with vivid details of his encounters with prostitutes. When I tried to change the subject, Jared would bring me back to his experiences with "hos," as he called them.

"Do you wear a condom?" I asked.

"Yeah, I do. You think I'm crazy!?" Jared came back, defensively.

I felt I had an obligation to discuss the risks of Jared's contracting HIV while he was having sex with prostitutes. I had questions in my mind as to whether or not Jared was using a condom, and it occurred to me that his having sex with prostitutes was perhaps his most dangerous behavior. Not the overdoses. Not the severe bouts of agitation that resulted in police calls in the middle of the night. But Jared insisted that he wore a condom every time, so I always left it at that.

Dr. Aptakar made sweeping changes to Jared's medication regimen. I liked working with Dr. Aptakar because he was more parsimonious in his approach to psychopharmacology than any psychiatrist I knew. At the time of my referral to Dr. Aptakar, Jared was on numerous medications from his previous psychiatrist. When I knew Jared in the 1980s, he seemed slow, drugged, and his speech was often slurred. He often complained of side effects, and it seemed that some of his hospitalizations were the result of iatrogenic effects of his medications. Dr. Aptakar took Jared off of most all of these medications and started him on a much simpler regimen. The results were remarkable. He had fewer side effects. His thoughts were clearer. He was more alert. He was more functional.

Jared and I met every week for the first month. Our sessions were organized around discussing his new medication regimen, reviewing his history, and discussing various stressors that arose between sessions. In our fourth session, we discussed Jared's history of numerous hospitalizations. Because he was 23-years-old, he had never gone more than 3 months without being hospitalized. His most recent hospitalization was 2 months ago. The following excerpt illustrates the formulation of a treatment goal that Jared and I coconstructed.

Counselor: How many times have you been in the hospital?

Client: A lot. So many, I can't remember. I think I figured out that I haven't gone more than 3 months without being admitted since my first time. So let me figure that out.

Counselor: Oh, that's okay. I can imagine it's a lot.

Client: No. Let me figure it out. Um. About 50 times? How is that?

Counselor: Fine.

Client: It's a lot.

Counselor: Now let me suggest something. Now you are with a new doctor. You are on new medication. It seems to be agreeing with you better. Maybe you don't need to go in the hospital as often.

Client: I was thinking the same thing.

Counselor: You were?

Client: I was thinking about it. Like now, I don't feel I need that. I feel very far away from that right now.

Counselor: Okay. What is different now?

Client: I'm not sure. Maybe it's the medication. The newness of everything. A new doctor and you. But I feel different.

Counselor: Okay. If something comes up, like a crisis or if you get upset, what might you do different?

Client: I don't know. I just think I might handle it different now.

Counselor: Okay. Have you gotten upset recently and handled it differently?

Client: I don't know. I can't think about that right now.

Counselor: Okay. That's fine.

Client: I just feel different now, like I don't need to go to the hospital. Like that's something from the past that I used to have to do. Maybe. We'll see.

Counselor: So would it make sense to you that one of the things we would agree to work on in our sessions is your finding ways to deal with life so that you don't have to go the hospital?

Client: Yeah, that makes sense to me.

In the preceding excerpt, I introduced to Jared the idea that he might not need to go to the hospital as often as he did in the past. Although solution-focused counseling aims to work on the client's goals, it also recognizes that counselors are active participants in the change process. Accordingly, so long as counselors maintain a collaborative relationship, they may introduce goals to the client. In this situation, Jared stated, "I was thinking the same thing." Jared then stated, "I feel very far away from that right now." I considered that Jared might be on the verge of identifying an exception regarding his ability to cope and the role of hospitalization in his life. I attempted to clarify his subjective feeling state by asking Jared, "What is different now?" Jared attributed his new feeling to the recent change in medication, having a new psychiatrist, and starting counseling with me.

Ideally, I would have preferred to direct Jared to look within himself for effective coping skills. Accordingly, I asked Jared to consider potential exceptions for dealing with a crisis that might have led to hospitalization in the past. Jared was unable to specify any such potential exceptions, so I didn't push it at this time. At the end of this session, however, we reached a consensus that a treatment goal would be for Jared to find ways of coping in order to avoid hospitalization. At the end of the session, I asked Jared to think about precisely what he will be doing when he is coping sufficiently better so that he seldom, if ever, requires hospitalization. I also asked him to observe for times when he was able to cope effectively in response to any stressor in his life. I wrote these tasks down on a piece of paper for Jared and asked that he record his observations in a notebook. We scheduled our next appointment in 2 weeks.

In the next series of counseling sessions, Jared tested my patience. One way he did this was to simply ignore my tasks. When I followed up in our next session to see what came of the task I gave him, Jared said that he didn't even remember my asking him to do it. Instead, he spent much of our current session reminiscing about his long psychiatric history and talking about the times he visited prostitutes. I tried to redirect Jared during the session on a number of occasions without success.

Jared did not show for our next appointment. When he called to reschedule, I informed him that per my policy he would be required to pay out of pocket for the previous session that he failed to cancel within 24 hours. Jared objected to my policy. He considered it to be too harsh. I explained the rationale of my policy. I pointed out that my time is worth money and if a client does not have the courtesy to cancel within 24 hours, then it is only fair to charge him or her my fee. Jared came back, "Okay. I guess I can deal with that. But it seems only fair that if *you* have to cancel one of our appointments in less than 24 hours that you should have to pay me your fee, too." I thought about it for a moment and came to the conclusion that Jared had made a logical argument. He was right. Jared's time was worthwhile, too. So I agreed with him, and we even put it in writing.

I was so impressed by Jared's comeback that I shared it with a colleague. My colleague thought it was absurd. She said that she would never enter into such an agreement with a client. "You are the counselor, and he is the client," she boldly affirmed. There was no use in trying to convince my colleague otherwise, but it was clear that she was drawing what de Shazer (1984) has referred to as a methodological boundary between the client and the counselor. This, I thought to myself, is the stuff that resistance is made of.

In our next session, I attempted to follow up on the task again. No luck. Jared reported that he had seen a prostitute a few days ago, and for this reason, he was in good spirits. Again, I asked Jared if he had used a condom. He responded, "Of course." I could have identified and amplified exceptions in relation to Jared's sexual experience with the prostitute, but thought that Jared had done pretty well for himself already in this regard. I listened patiently as Jared went on and on about the prostitute. He had a look of glee on his face as he described what he referred to as "the one joy in my life."

Jared cancelled our next appointment, this time within the required 24-hour period. Then I didn't hear from Jared for about a week. So I left a message for Jared to call me to reschedule. A month passed, and then Jared called me in a crisis.

"I hate my parents!" he said. "I hate them!"

Jared told me on the phone that he got into a big argument with his parents after his car broke down. He now feared that *he* was going to break down. I couldn't get the whole story from Jared on the phone, but I asked him whether he thought it would be helpful if his parents joined us for a session. Jared was hesitant at first but then agreed. We set an appointment for the same day with Jared and his parents.

Jared's parents were in their 60s. His father was very quiet. His mother did most of the talking during the session. His mother stated that she and her husband had bought Jared a used car 4 years ago. They constantly reminded Jared to take care of the car, to take it to the shop for maintenance, and that sort of thing, but it was always an uphill battle like everything else. Yesterday, Jared called his parents and told them that the car broke down on the highway. This morning the repair shop said that the engine was completely shot. There was no oil in the engine. There was a slow oil leak, and Jared hadn't gotten an oil change in over a year.

"I have had it!" his mother yelled. "If you only knew what we've been through with Jared through the years. We have died a hundred times. And we're *not* getting him another car!" She turned to Jared and screamed, "You can take the bus now!"

Jared had been sitting quietly in the chair listening to his mother's tirade. He was visibly calm. And then he erupted, like a volcano, and yelled loudly, "Screw the car!" Jared's mother began to cry. His father put his arm around his wife and looked at me. He had deep lines in his face, and with a sad grin asked me, "Doctor, can you help Jared?" Jared sat calmly in the chair and avoided eye contact with anyone in the room. I took a deep breath and suggested that Jared and I continue to work together. "What do you think, Jared?" I asked. "That's fine," he replied. We scheduled our next appointment 2 days later.

Prior to our next appointment, it dawned on me that it had been about 3 months since Jared was hospitalized. He was approaching a milestone because he had never gone so long between admissions. I was determined in our next session to help Jared focus on what he was doing to keep himself out of the hospital. If Jared wouldn't do the solution-focused tasks that I gave him between the sessions, then I would at least try to enact them during the sessions. I was relieved when I saw Jared sitting in my waiting room for our next session because I feared he might have decompensated since our prior meeting.

Counselor: So what's happened since I saw you last time?

Client: Not much. The car is gone.

Counselor: How did you get here?

Client: My mother drove me.

Counselor: I thought you were going to take the bus.

Client: Yeah, I take the bus. But she thinks this is important, so she wanted to drive me.

Counselor: Okay. I understand.

Client: Whatever. Yeah. But I would have come by bus.

Counselor: Good. So let me ask you something. I was a little worried there when we had your parents here last time.

Client: What, that? Nah! It's nothing.

Counselor: Well, it didn't seem like nothing.

Client: They were freaked out as usual.

Counselor: But were you freaked out as usual?

Client: No I was not!

Counselor: You used to be.

Client: Damn right.

Counselor: This time, though, you weren't.

Client: No. No way.

Counselor: Why not?

Client: I told myself, "Screw it. It's not freaking worth it."

Counselor: That's something.

Client: What?

Counselor: To say, "Screw it. It's not worth it."

Client: It's not.

Counselor: To say that is one thing. But to believe that strongly is another. People give lip service to things all the time, but they don't believe it and they don't act on it as if they believe it.

Client: Well, I believed it. And I still do. Screw it.

Counselor: I think if we talk about this idea you have, this "It's not worth it" idea, it might give us a better sense of how you are able to hold it together when things are stressful. Do you know what I mean?

Client: Yeah. I know what you mean.

Counselor: I think it's a good way you came up with to cope.

When I look back now, I see that this was a turning point in counseling with Jared. In the preceding excerpt, I asked Jared why he had not freaked out in response to his car breaking down and his parents getting upset. He replied, "Screw it. It's not freaking worth it." I then attempted to show the client that this was a significant and effective coping skill that he used in response to a stressful situation. My next step in this session was to amplify this exception, that is, help Jared identify differences between the times when he was unable to cope effectively and the times when he did.

Mastering the Art of Solution-Focused Counseling

Counselor: How did you come up with that idea, "It's not worth it?"

Client: I don't know.

Counselor: Well . . .

Client: I've thought it before, but not that much. I just came up with it.

Counselor: Okay.

Client: I guess I realized that it's not that bad. It is bad, the car is busted. That's bad. But it's not that bad.

Counselor: Right.

Client: It's that if I get upset it's only going to make it worse.

Counselor: Ah. That's smart. Okay. So you convinced yourself of the logic of it, that it's not worth getting upset about.

Client: It's worth being upset about, but not off the wall. I don't need to go the hospital because my car broke down.

Counselor: Okay. That makes a lot of sense. Now let me ask you another question.

Client: Yeah.

Counselor: We see now that you came up with this way to cope, to say, "It's not worth it."

Client: Right.

Counselor: If we can, let's look at how this is different from how you might have responded in the past?

Client: I would have gotten all freaked out.

Counselor: In what way?

Client: Oh, I don't know. I might have screamed a lot or yelled at my mother. I might have run around. Sometimes I don't remember half the shit I did.

Counselor: Hmm.

Client: I think I'm different now.

Counselor: In what way?

Client: A lot of it is the medication. I can think better now.

Counselor: Okay.

Client: But I also think I'm doing better.

Counselor: I agree. So given that the medication is working better, you can think better now, and you can cope better now, what do you think this says about the future?

Client: Better. I don't even think much about going to the hospital anymore.

In this excerpt, I was able to help the client amplify the exception, "It's not worth it." We agreed that he reached a logical conclusion that it is not worth getting himself upset. We also contrasted the exception with his prior ineffective coping methods. Finally, the client attributed his change to the new medication, being able to think more clearly, and changes that he was making himself. I could see that a new identity was emerging for Jared when he stated, "I don't even think much about going to the hospital anymore."

A NEW BEGINNING

A year had passed since I started seeing Jared. He still had occasional crises, but still no hospitalizations. We continued to focus on Jared's exceptional coping skills during our sessions. Sometimes we met twice a month or less frequently. Then, for a new year's resolution, Jared stated that his goal was to get off all medication. At the time, Jared was prescribed Haldol (an antipsychotic), Zoloft (an antidepressant), and Ativan (a benzodiazepine). I was interested in the idea of Jared getting off medication. I frequently wonder about people who take psychotropic medications—antipsychotic drugs, in particular—for years. They are sedated and in some cases chemically restrained. So many clients complain of side effects. And most of the time they are either noncompliant or do not take the medication properly. It seems that in some cases the solution has become the problem. At first I was leery of Jared's motives. Upon questioning him, however, he expressed a desire to feel "more normal." He said that he felt too sedated on the Haldol and that it was holding him back from moving forward in his life. Jared was serious and determined. I also thought it was wise for Jared to raise the issue in counseling rather than just stopping the medication on his own, and I complimented him for this. So I suggested that he consider doing so only if his psychiatrist Dr. Aptakar agreed and would monitor him during the process. Jared agreed to this plan.

I called Dr. Aptakar, and we discussed the possibility of Jared being taken off his medication. Dr. Aptakar told me that in his experience it was rare for a person with schizophrenia to function satisfactorily without medication. I told Dr. Aptakar that Jared raised the question of stopping his medication during one of our counseling sessions and that I thought this was better than if he had just stopped on his own. I told the psychiatrist that Jared seemed determined to get off the medication. I asked if Dr. Aptakar could at least be available to monitor him during the process. Dr. Aptakar reluctantly agreed to the plan.

Dr. Aptakar tapered Jared off the Haldol. Jared seldom took the Ativan, so this was immediately discontinued. He remained on the Zoloft because Dr. Aptakar felt it was helping his depression. I met with Jared on a weekly basis at Dr. Aptakar's request during that first month when the Haldol was being tapered. Jared seemed fine. For the next month, he denied hallucinations, there was no evidence of delusions, and I did not detect any psychotic thought process. He had his moments of agitation from time to time. So Dr. Aptakar refilled the prescription for Ativan so he could calm himself as needed. But it seemed that Jared's psychosis was in remission.

Nine months passed with Jared off the Haldol. He continued to be free of psychotic symptoms. His mother bought him another used car, which he was now determined to take care of. In fact, Jared was almost obsessive about following the recommended maintenance schedule for the car. He had not been hospitalized since we began counseling almost 2 years ago. Following is an excerpt from a session we had at this time in which we coconstructed a new problem and goal.

Client: I was listening to something on the radio the other day while I was driving. It was about road rage.

Counselor: Road rage?

Client: Yeah. You know, when people get upset while they are behind the wheel.

Counselor: Right.

Client: It was very interesting. They had an expert being interviewed, and he said that there are two types of people on the road. There is the type that goes crazy when they are stuck in traffic and then there is the second type. The second type does not go crazy.

Counselor: The second type probably accepts that it will take a certain amount of time to get to work. They know it takes that amount of time, maybe a little longer, maybe sooner.

Client: Right.

Counselor: And they don't make themselves crazy if they get in a traffic jam.

Client: Right. Those are the two types of people. I realized that I am the first type.

Counselor: You are the type that makes yourself crazy?

Client: Right.

Counselor: The first type or the second type?

Client: I am not the second type, the type who accepts it.

Counselor: Okay.

Client: I realized that I'm not one of those people.

Counselor: Maybe not.

Client: And that's my problem. I'm not really normal.

Counselor: But wait a minute. What is normal? There are many people who are the first type. I am the first type in a way.

Client: You are?

Counselor: Yes. It's not good for me. And I try to work on it. But I make myself needlessly upset when I get stuck in traffic and for many other nuisances that happen in life, waiting in lines at the store, any little thing. So I also do that. But I try to work on it and do better because it is a problem, like you say.

Client: Okay. But this is the thing. It's not just the road rage.

Counselor: I know. It's other things. It's many things.

Client: No, no, no. It's something bigger.

Counselor: Describe it to me, then.

Client: I've told you all of my life how I felt.

Counselor: Right.

Client: I wish I could tell you. I've had it within me all my life, and I can't shake it.

Counselor: Can you describe it some more to me?

Client: I guess, but it's probably not worth it. It never gets me anywhere. I'm talked out about it. There's really nothing I can do to change it. It's the thing I have inside of me that makes me feel bad about myself.

Counselor: What you have told me?

Client: Yeah.

Counselor: For all you have done?

Client: For being sick, being on disability, being a failure. I made my parents unhappy. All I can tell you is that ever since I was a boy I felt this thing in me.

Counselor: Yeah.

Client: The feeling of being a loser. I can't even find the words to describe it. It's more like a feeling. There aren't any words. And it brings me down.

Counselor: How does it bring you down now?

Client: Not down like it used to. I'm not the same anymore. I'm not going to freak out, or I hope not. Or I'm not going to call the police or go the hospital or anything over it.

Counselor: But it has you feeling down.

Client: Yeah. I'm sad about my life. I'm unhappy.

Counselor: You said that you aren't the same anymore. What do you mean?

Client: I said already that I'm not going psychotic anymore. I'm different now.

Counselor: You *are* different.

Client: [Crying] I want to be different.

Counselor: Tell me how you would be. If you were different.

Client: Oh, I would be like the other type of person. On that radio show where the guy said there are two types of people. You know?

Counselor: Yeah. The second one.

Client: Right. The second type. I wish I was like that one. Calm and normal. Happy. But I'm not.

Counselor: Maybe not. But maybe you are like the second type in some ways some of the time.

Client: No way. Never. It's not me.

Counselor: No? Okay.

Client: I'm this loser that can't do much about it but be a loser.

Counselor: Hmm.

Client: There is one thing I can do about it.

Counselor: What's that?

Client: I can go to hoes.

Counselor: The prostitutes.

Client: Right.

Counselor: You might be able to make it with normal women if you tried, but you haven't given yourself a chance from what I see.

Client: Nah! It's not worth it. I go to hoes and I'm telling you, it's my one enjoyment.

Counselor: Okay. So even though you're a loser, as you put it, you can find some pleasure.

Client: Yeah, and no one is going to take that away from me.

Counselor: Okay. You enjoy it. What else gives you pleasure?

Client: Not much.
Counselor: Okay.
Client: My car, I guess.
Counselor: Your car.
Client: Yeah, I guess.
Counselor: What about the car?
Client: I take care of it now. It's not a chore. I like to.
Counselor: So you enjoy caring for the car?
Client: Yeah.

In this excerpt, Jared referred to a radio program in which a distinction was drawn between two types of people: people who get upset in traffic jams and people who do not get upset in traffic jams. Jared identified himself with the former. I suggested to Jared, "Maybe you are like the second type in some ways some of the time." But Jared insisted, "No way. Never. It's not me." Accordingly, I accepted his claim that he was the first type of person. Jared went on to describe a problem that he has had within him for all of his life. He stated, "It's the thing I have inside of me that makes me feel bad about myself." At this point, Jared was talking about his relationship to his self. He described himself as a loser. The conversation then shifted to ways in which he is able to find pleasure in life despite his feeling like a loser. The excerpt that follows corresponds to a later stage during the same session.

Client: I'm starting to see now.
Counselor: What's that?
Client: This is making sense to me now.
Counselor: How is that?
Client: Well, this feeling I have of being a loser, right?
Counselor: Right.
Client: I doubt I'll ever shake it. Do you?
Counselor: Do I?
Client: Do you think I'll shake it?
Counselor: I don't know.
Client: I don't think so. That's me.
Counselor: Okay. I'm not sure you *really* are a loser, but you really have this feeling of being a loser.
Client: Yeah.
Counselor: Okay, I'll buy that. So let's suppose you're right. You have this experience.
Client: Well, I'm a nut.
Counselor: You're a nut?
Client: Yeah. I doubt I'm ever going to really shake this feeling. So I might as well accept it.
Counselor: Accept the feeling?
Client: I guess.

Counselor: Maybe accept that you have this feeling of being a loser, that you might never shake it because it's part of who you are—not being a loser, but having this feeling of being a loser—and maybe then going on and trying to enjoy your life despite the feeling.

Client: Right.

Counselor: It's sort of like surrendering to it.

Client: Yeah. I can surrender to it.

Counselor: So you can cope with the feeling of being a loser and accept having the feeling and try to enjoy yourself despite the feeling or even with it.

Client: Right. Like when I go to hoes.

Counselor: Right. And there might be other things that you will enjoy doing. You mentioned caring for your car. There might be other things, too.

Jared initiated the idea of accepting his feeling of being a loser. I then introduced the goal of Jared accepting his feeling of being a loser and trying to enjoy his life despite having this feeling. From a solution-focused perspective, Jared's complaint (viewing his self as a loser) paired with the exception of accepting this feeling and working toward pleasure despite it resulted in a salient completion of the problem/solution distinction.

In 1997, Jared died of a heart attack.

CONCLUDING REMARKS

In this chapter, a case example was provided to exemplify the theory and practice of solution-focused counseling. I learned a lot from Jared. I learned about the importance of believing in the client. In my heart and in my mind, I always strived to accept Jared as a human being. I tried not to think of Jared as a chronic mental patient, or a schizophrenic, or even the loser that he thought of himself. I viewed him as a normal person, and I think he sensed this. I also learned to practice patience. Jared and I spent many hours talking. Most of the time, I just listened. Sometimes I didn't know where our talk would take us. Sometimes it seemed to take us nowhere. But sometimes it took us to wondrous places. Most of all, I learned about possibility. Dr. Aptakar and I both thought it was remarkable that Jared functioned as well as he did without the Haldol. Jared even considered pursuing vocational training so that he could eventually go back to work. I still often think about Jared, and he will always be an inspiration to me.

Mastering the Art of Solution-Focused Counseling

CHAPTER 11
The Future of Solution-Focused Counseling

Given the emphasis that solution-focused counseling places on possibility, it seems only fitting to end this book with a discussion about the future. So what can we expect in the future and beyond—in the world, in the counseling profession, and for solution-focused counseling? The problem with this question is that we can only see so far into the future. Our visions are limited by a horizon that is based on our current frames of reference. For example, Sigmund Freud considered emotional disturbance to be so deeply rooted biologically that he imagined a day when disorders would be treated most efficiently with psychotropic medications (Gay, 1988). But it is questionable whether Freud might have imagined the many other developments that came into fruition in the many years since his death. In this chapter, I describe new directions for solution-focused counseling.

NEW DIRECTIONS FOR SOLUTION-FOCUSED COUNSELING

In this section, I describe three significant developments for solution-focused counseling: (a) the role of emotions in solution-focused theory and practice, (b) efforts to expand the settings in which solution-focused principles are applied, and (c) influences of a technological society for solution-focused counseling.

The Role of Emotions in Solution-Focused Counseling

An increasing literature has addressed the important role of emotions in solution-focused theory and practice (Kiser, Piercy, & Lipchik, 1993; Lipchik, 2002;

Piercy, Lipchik, & Kiser, 2000). In particular, it has been suggested that emotional issues are traditionally not emphasized in solution-focused models (Kiser et al., 1993; Lipchik, 2002; Piercy et al., 2000). According to Piercy et al. (2000), some clinicians misinterpret the brief, minimalist, and pragmatic strategies of solution-focused models and, as a result, neglect processing painful feeling states that clients might experience:

> Solution-focused clinicians need to know how to acknowledge, join with, and respond to client emotions as well as thoughts and actions . . . . We believe it **to be** helpful to reframe emotions as strengths. But not all negative emotions should be talked away in therapy. Sometimes it is best simply to be with clients in their despair, grief, or depression . . . . Thus, we need not always find exceptions or too quickly move away from such emotions. Feeling talk can sometimes be the best solution talk . . . . The development of a more emotion-rich solution-focused therapy, we believe, will bring an important dimension to this therapy. (p. 26)

Miller and de Shazer (2000) have set forth an alternative conceptualization that incorporates philosopher Wittgenstein's (1963) language games and rule-following as a basis from which to develop a solution-focused orientation to emotions. According to Miller and de Shazer, "when clients talk about emotions and problems, they are following the rules of problem-focused language games. Shifting to a solution-focused language game will provide clients with new 'emotion rules' to follow, and new forms of life for experiencing emotions" (2000, p. 17). In a response to Miller and de Shazer (2000), Piercy et al. (2000) have provided the following critique:

> Their presentation of solution-focused therapy as a Wittgenstein language game seems unnecessarily cognitive and detached from human experience. In privileging the head over the heart, the authors succeed in avoiding intimate struggles in therapy. But at what price? Solution-focused therapists who fail to connect on an emotional level with their clients, we believe, are less effective. Moreover, Miller and de Shazer's methods place the therapist in a rather noncollaborative, expert role. From our point of view, this language-game approach to emotions will be less than satisfying for most therapists and clients. (pp. 27–28)

Although there is a lack of consensus among theorists regarding the role of emotions in solution-focused approaches (cf. Miller & de Shazer, 2000; Piercy et al., 2000), recent attempts to integrate this aspect of human experience into the models is a good sign. Solution-focused counseling holds promise to extend the work in this area. By virtue of its strategic approach to eclecticism (see chapter 3), solution-focused counseling is able to incorporate the formal content from various clinical theories within its change process and thereby address emotions in various ways. For example, it might be fitting in some cases to emphasize clarification, reflection, and understanding of feelings and therefore incorporate a person-centered approach within the change process. In some cases, it might be more helpful to use a gestalt approach to help clients increase their awareness of feelings. In other cases, cognitive–behavioral strategies (e.g., REBT) might be employed to help clients identify and dispute irrational beliefs that theoretically cause disruptive emotions.

In solution-focused counseling, one of the principal criteria for the selection of any given technique is a fit with the client's worldview, including the client's understanding of the problem, expectations of counseling, and goals of treatment. Emotions will inevitably play different roles in different cases. Accordingly, flexibility and creativity on the part of counselors will continue to be a key to successful outcome.

New Settings for Solution-Focused Counseling

Solution-focused therapy was originally developed in the 1980s at the Brief Family Therapy Center in Milwaukee, Wisconsin. The Center is an outpatient mental health setting where clinical services are provided to individuals, couples, and families, and training and supervision is provided to students and professionals. In the 1990s, solution-focused approaches were applied in various traditional mental health settings, including community mental health centers, private practice, and psychiatric hospitals. Recently, however, there have been increasing efforts to expand the settings in which solution-focused models can be successfully applied. Following is a description of solution-focused applications that have been increasingly applied in several new settings.

A review of the literature indicates that solution-focused models have been successfully applied in school settings. School counselors have applied solution-focused approaches to various educational levels, including elementary school (Sklare, 2005), middle and high school (Murphy, 1997), and college (Santa, 1995). Solution-focused models have been applied to a variety of clinical problems in schools, including bullying (Young & Holdore, 2003), family dysfunction (Doerries & Foster, 2001), and disasters and trauma (Klingman, 2002). In addition, these models have been used by teachers and school administrators in a variety of ways. For example, Casey (2002) has set forth a school curriculum that incorporates solution-focused principles to help students achieve behavioral goals, cope with disruptive feelings, and manage interpersonal conflicts.

School counselors, teachers, and administrators will continue to play a critical role as change agents in increasingly complex educational school systems. Accordingly, it has become necessary for schools to develop innovative and effective strategies to bring about change in school settings. For many schools, solution-focused approaches have been adopted as a conceptual foundation for addressing many clinical and programmatic needs.

Solution-focused principles have also been applied to the area of organizational consultation. In the past decade, there has been an increase in the use of consultants for organizations, including the private business sector and nonprofit organizations. Increasingly, executives, managers, team leaders, and employees are seeking the services of consultants to solve problems, create change, and improve performances (Burke, 2002). A proliferation of solution-focused consultation approaches has emerged following the appreciative inquiry movement (Cooperrider, Sorensen, Yaeger, & Whitney, 2004), a human resource management approach to organizational change. Solution-focused consultation usually aims to help staff groups enhance a greater sense of teamwork and commitment to the organization by applying the model's strength-based principles. The application of solution-focused models to organizations is still in its infancy, and hence there is a paucity of literature that documents these efforts. Nevertheless, an increasing number of solution-focused consultants have recently emerged. The Brief Family Therapy Center, the clinic where solution-focused therapy was developed, offers consultation to organizations. The Helsinki Brief Therapy Institute offers a solution-focused organizational approach called Reteaming. In addition, an increasing number of practitioners are now including solution-focused consultation among the services they provide. Similar to appreciative inquiry and its positive approach to organizational change, it appears that solution-focused applications to consultation fill a need for brief, effective, and strength-based intervention in the workplace.

I conclude this section by highlighting the self-help movement. Unlike the other settings just described (schools, organizations), self-help pervades society. It has no place and, instead, permeates virtually all aspects of our lives. Increasingly, solution-focused principles have been introduced into the self-help market. Accordingly, it is worth mentioning here this important development.

Norcross (2000) has warned that "a massive, systemic, and yet largely silent revolution is occurring in mental health today and is gathering steam for tomorrow: self-help efforts without professional intervention" (p. 370). Self-help books top the best-seller lists. Millions of television viewers are turning to Dr. Phil for advice. And now even prominent theorists and practitioners are telling us that self-help factors contribute most to successful outcome in counseling and psychotherapy (e.g., Ellis, 1997b; Norcross, 2000).

Self-help comes in many forms. Books. Support groups. The Internet. Religious and spiritual activities. Self-management programs. Herbal remedies. *Anything* that involves finding a way to somehow change behavior. Norcross (2000) has attributed the self-help revolution to various factors. First, a large number of counselors and psychotherapists recommend self-help activities to their clients as an adjunct to professional treatment. Second, self-help works! Third, self-help is less expensive than professional treatment and is often just as effective. Gergen (1994) has noted that "as various cultural interest groups gain common consciousness in the 21st century, psychology's claims to a superior voice will be increasingly thrust into question" (p. 413).

So what is a counselor and, in particular, a solution-focused counselor to do? I recommend that we embrace the self-help movement lest we miss the forthcoming revolution. Efforts to adapt to the self-help movement are apparent. A new discipline called coaching has emerged. Coaching is designed to help one reach his or her full potential, strive for self-actualization, and create an extraordinary life. I am not suggesting that you necessarily become a coach like Tony Robbins (1997). But perhaps there are some lessons to be learned from this movement. Futurist Alvin Toffler (1970, 1980) has predicted that a new profession—called *life planning*—will replace today's traditional counseling and psychotherapy. According to Toffler, rather than help clients resolve their intrapsychic conflicts or emotional problems, life planners will assist people with more practical concerns such as balancing their budgets, finding affordable housing, getting a job, meeting new friends, and so forth.

Solution-focused counseling is well suited for self-help and life planning strategies because it is a self-help system. The essence of the model is based on the principle that clients have existing strengths, natural resources, and problem-solving capabilities that they bring to treatment. Solution-focused counseling is informed by the theory that change is produced when clients are encouraged to identify and enact these preexisting self-help resources. The eclectic model used in solution-focused counseling also allows for the introduction of self-help materials to supplement as needed the client's repertoire of problem-solving skills. Already, a number of authors have written self-help books that specifically explicate solution-focused principles for the layperson (e.g., B. O'Hanlon, 2004; Weiner-Davis, 1993).

As the self-help movement continues to grow, I recommend that counselors consider how their roles might be shaped by this inevitable trend. As Norcross (2000) has noted, the self-help movement is here to stay:

> [We] can idly watch with bemused interest—devaluing self-change as shallow, self-help books as trivial, and Internet sites as harmless—as the train roars past us. Alternatively, we can recognize the power and potential of the locomotive and help steer it to valuable destinations for our . . . [clients] and the populace. (p. 376)

Technological Society and Solution-Focused Counseling

The most precious commodity today is information. Although we are still influenced to a large degree by the first two waves that were developed in society—agriculture and industry—the third wave—technology—has taken over (Toffler, 1980). The Internet is no longer an esoteric form of mass media. It has become a daily necessity for anyone who wishes to quickly send data to other people, do research online, and have access to the latest information in the world. Some counselors are already providing online services to clients (Guterman & Kirk, 1999). In 1997, the International Society for Mental Health Online was formed to promote the development of online communication, information, and technology for the international mental health community. Distance education and training has also become widespread in counselor education and related fields (e.g., Altekruse & Brew, 2000; Bobby & Capone, 2000).

I have been an active contributor to the Internet since 1995. From the beginning, I was astonished by the similarities between the Internet and postmodernism. Postmodernism holds that realities—including those that derive from our theories of counseling and client–counselor interactions—are the result of collaboration and social consensus. Along similar lines, the Internet affords virtually everyone an opportunity to make their voice heard. Almost anyone can create a Web site. If you are not interested in creating a Web site, then it is possible to contribute by posting comments on bulletin boards, electronic mailing lists, or on someone else's Web site. Indeed, the Internet sets forth endless possibilities for much needed dialogue in our profession.

Also in keeping with postmodernism is the active role that users play on the Internet. Unlike other forms of mass media in which one is a passive recipient of what is read, heard, or viewed, users of the Internet are participant–observers who interact with and thereby change the content. Like counselors in this postmodern era, users of the Internet both influence and are influenced by the observed. Furthermore, ideas on the Internet are fluid, rather than fixed, and thus the only constant is change. This means that advances in counseling can be instantly disseminated. Could this be the beginning of the end of publication lag? When an article is accepted for publication by a scholarly journal, it can sometimes take 1 year or longer for it to be published due to the backlog of already accepted manuscripts. As a result, a number of peer-reviewed online journals have been developed in recent years.

Furthermore, the Internet changes how we share information. Unlike the sequential order of the text in books, the images on television, and the sounds on radio, the Internet provides users with potentially infinite choices via links. There are also many search engines that link to Web sites on virtually any topic. On the World Wide Web, when you click on a link (denoted by a word or phrase that is usually underlined), you are taken to another page or an altogether different site that, in turn, includes links to other resources (and so on). Hence, much of the Internet is a collaborative effort and full of potentially infinite resources.

The Internet and its technology is particularly conducive to the goals of solution-focused counseling. If we understand solution-focused counseling as holding a place within the self-help movement, then technology will play an integral role. It is feasible to use e-mail and other Internet applications to conduct solution-focused counseling (Collie, Mitchell, & Murphy, 2000). Now the miracle question can be asked with a simple keystroke.

An ambitious use of technology for solution-focused purposes has been realized by Family Solutions, a nonprofit counseling and community services agency. Family Solutions has several offices in Summit County, Ohio, and has adopted an agency wide solution-focused approach. In 1999, Family Solutions received a grant to bring computers and the Internet to public housing and other organizations in need. The grant has been used to create community technology centers to serve young people and adults in two locations in Metropolitan Housing Authority locations in Akron, Ohio. The community technology centers opened in 2000 to make the benefits of computers and the Internet available to those who cannot afford them. Anyone who lives or works in Summit County, Ohio, is eligible to use the centers on a drop-in basis. In addition, numerous established Family Solutions vocational programs are offered at these sites. The work being done by Family Solutions exemplifies the possibilities when technology is used to help those in need. It goes beyond merely talking about solutions and, instead, creates the very context in which people can grow. Similar to Toffler's (1970, 1980) vision of life planning, such endeavors serve to bridge the digital divide that is widening the gap between the haves and the have-nots in society.

We are just beginning to realize the influences of technology in society and counseling. In the next decade, many of us will be donned with fully functioning, wearable computers (Siewiorek & Hamilton, 2003). And then there will be the *singularity* (Kurzweil, 2005). Some futurists speculate that in the future the pace of technological development will become so rapid that the rate of progress will become almost vertical. Then, in a short period of time (months, days, hours, even seconds), the world will be transformed beyond recognition. This point is referred to as the singularity. The cause of a singularity would be the creation of some form of rapidly self-enhancing greater-than-human artificial intelligence (AI). A singularity is likely to happen as a result of advances in the development of AI and complex systems of networked computers. A positive feedback loop will ensue whereby smarter computers are able to design even smarter computers (and so forth). This loop would be so rapid and sudden that real AI would emerge.

There is debate regarding precisely when the singularity will occur. Some experts think it will happen in about 100 years. Some think it will occur sometime in the next 50 years. But all agree that the singularity and AI *will* happen. And when it does, the world and humanity will be changed beyond our wildest imaginations. There will be a new type of being—something we can now only envision as a future being—that will live among us. Referred to by many as *posthuman*, these beings would be completely synthetic. They will be robots, if you will. But not of the ilk we have become accustomed to in science fiction. Posthumans will be able to share their experiences with one another directly. They will be able to transmute their bodies into data forms and choose to temporarily, or permanently, reside in computer networks. They will be able to think, feel, and behave very much as real people do. It is difficult for humans to comprehend what the life of a posthuman might be. But it is not a stretch to imagine a world in which posthumans and humans coexist. The implications for counseling are nontrivial if we consider the potential scenarios when super-intelligent robots come to be. *Robotic counselors. Miracle uploading. Virtual solutions.* These are some of the possibilities that lie just beyond the horizon.

FINAL REMARKS

No matter how the world might change, I am confident that some things will remain constant. Regardless of the technological advances in society, there will still be people in the world. Real living breathing people. And there will still be human problems. The future will bring new challenges, and in many ways we are not prepared to deal with the changes that are forthcoming. Many people are already in a state of future shock (Toffler, 1970). Regardless of self-help, it is clear that people will always need people to help them cope with and find solutions to their problems of daily living. So for now and for the immediate future, it is certain that counselors will continue to be needed in our ever changing society.

In this book, I have set forth solution-focused counseling as a comprehensive clinical model to help clients resolve their problems in an effective and efficient manner. Although I have attempted to address the many potential clinical applications of solution-focused counseling, this model is by no means complete; it is a work in progress. I look forward to developing this model further with my colleagues, students, and clients as we endeavor to practice mastering the art of solution-focused counseling.

REFERENCES

Allgood, S. M., Parham, K. B., Salts, C. J., & Smith, T. A. (1995). The association between pretreatment change and unplanned termination in family therapy. *American Journal of Family Therapy, 23,* 195–202.

Altekruse, M. K., & Brew, L. (2000). Using the Web for distance learning. In J. W. Bloom & G. R. Walz (Eds.), *Cybercounseling and cyberlearning: Strategies and resources for the millennium* (pp. 129–141). Alexandria, VA: American Counseling Association/ERIC CASS.

American Counseling Association. (2005). *ACA code of ethics.* Alexandria, VA: Author.

American Psychiatric Association. (2000). *Diagnostic and statistical manual of mental disorders* (4th ed., text rev.). Washington, DC: Author.

Anderson, H. (1996). *Conversation, language, and possibilities: A postmodern approach to therapy.* New York: Basic Books.

Anderson, H., & Goolishian, H. A. (1988). Human systems as linguistic systems: Preliminary and evolving ideas about the implications for clinical theory. *Family Process, 27,* 371–393.

Anderson, H., Goolishian, H., Pulliam, G., & Winderman, L. (1986). The Galveston Family Institute: Some personal and historical perspectives. In D. E. Efron (Ed.), *Journeys: Expansion of the strategic-systemic therapies* (pp. 97–122). New York: Brunner/Mazel.

Anderson, W. T. (1990). *Reality isn't what it used to be: Theatrical politics, ready-to-wear religion, global myths, primitive chic, and other wonders of the postmodern world.* San Francisco: Harper & Row.

Azocar, F., Cuffel, B., & Goldman, W. (2003). The impact of evidence-based guideline dissemination for the assessment and treatment of major depression in a managed behavioral health care organization. *Journal of Behavioral Health Services and Research, 30*(1), 109–118.

Bandura, A. (Ed.). (1997). *Self-efficacy in changing societies.* Cambridge, MA: Cambridge University Press.

Bateson, G. (1972). *Steps to an ecology of mind.* New York: Ballantine.

Bateson, G. (1979). *Mind and nature: A necessary unity.* New York: Dutton.

Bateson, G., Jackson, D. D., Haley, J., & Weakland, J. (1956). Toward a theory of schizophrenia. *Behavioral Science, 2,* 154–161.

Beattie, M. (1996). *Codependent no more: How to stop controlling others and start caring for yourself* (2nd ed.). Center City, MN: Hazelden.

Beck, A. T. (1976). *Cognitive therapy and the emotional disorders*. New York: International Universities Press.

Berkeley, G. (1963). A *treatise concerning the principles of human knowledge*. La Salle, IL: Open Court.

Berg, I. K. (1989). Of visitors, complainants, and customers. Is there really such thing as resistance? *Family Therapy Networker, 13*(1), 21.

Berg, I. K., & Miller, S. D. (1992). *Working with the problem drinker: A solution-focused approach*. New York: Norton.

Berger, P., & Luckmann, T. (1967). *The social construction of reality*. Garden City, NY: Doubleday.

Bishay, N. R., Tarrier, N., & Dolan, M. (1996). Morbid jealousy: A cognitive outlook. *Journal of Cognitive Psychotherapy, 10*, 9–22.

Blocher, D. H. (1989). What's in a name: Reactions to Hershenson et al. *Journal of Mental Health Counseling, 11*, 70–76.

Bobby, C. L., & Capone, L. (2000). Understanding the implications of distance learning for accreditation and licensure of counselor preparation programs. In J. W. Bloom & G. R. Walz (Eds.), *Cybercounseling and cyberlearning: Strategies and resources for the millennium* (pp. 361–377). Alexandria, VA: American Counseling Association/ERIC CASS.

Boscolo, L., Cecchin, C., Hoffman, L., & Penn, P. (1987). *Milan systemic family therapy*. New York: Basic Books.

Bruner, J. (1986). *Actual minds, possible worlds*. Cambridge, MA: Harvard University Press.

Burke, W. W. (2002). *Organizational change: Theory and practice*. Thousand, Oaks, CA: Sage.

Butler, W. R., & Powers, K. V. (1996). Solution-focused grief therapy. In S. D. Miller, M. A. Hubble, & B. L. Duncan (Eds.), *Handbook of solution-focused brief therapy* (pp. 228–247). San Francisco: Jossey-Bass.

Byrd, M. R., Richards, D. F., & Hove, G. (2002). Treatment of early onset hair pulling as a simple habit. *Behavior Modification, 26*, 400–411.

Casey, J. (2002). *Getting it right: A behaviour curriculum*. Bristol, England: Lucky Duck.

Chilvers, C., Dewey, M., Fielding, K., Gretton, V., Miller, P., & Palmer, N. (2001). Antidepressant drugs and generic counseling for treatment of major depression in primary care. *British Medical Journal, 322*, 772–775.

Collie, K. R., Mitchell, D., & Murphy, L. (2000). Skills for online counseling: Maximum impact at minimum bandwidth. In J. W. Bloom & G. R. Walz (Eds.), *Cybercounseling and cyberlearning: Strategies and resources for the millennium* (pp. 219–236). Alexandria, VA: American Counseling Association/ERIC CASS.

Cooperrider, D. L., Sorensen, P. F., Yaeger, T. F., & Whitney, D. (Eds.). (2004). *Appreciative inquiry: An emerging direction for organization development*. Champaign, IL: Stripes.

Cottrell, D., & Boston, P. (2002). Practitioner review: The effectiveness of systemic family therapy for children and adolescents. *Journal of Child Psychology and Psychiatry, 43*, 573–586.

Cox, B. J., Enns, M. W., & Clara, I. P. (2004). Psychological dimensions associated with suicidal ideations and attempts in the National Comorbidity Survey. *Suicide and Life-Threatening Behavior, 34*, 209–219.

Culler, J. (1982). *On deconstruction.* Ithaca, NY: Cornell University Press.

Dahl, R., Bathel, D., & Carreon, C. (2000). The use of solution-focused therapy with an elderly population. *Journal of Systemic Therapies, 19*(4), 45–55.

D'Andrea, M. (2000). Postmodernism, constructivism, and multiculturalism: Three forces reshaping and expanding our thoughts about counseling. *Journal of Mental Health Counseling, 22*, 1–16.

Davy, J. (1999). Constructionist approaches to bereavement and therapy: Part 2. *Counseling Psychology Review, 14*(1), 3–11.

de Shazer, S. (1978). Brief hypnotherapy of two sexual dysfunctions: The Crystal Ball Technique. *American Journal of Clinical Hypnosis, 20*, 203–208.

de Shazer, S. (1982). *Patterns of brief family therapy.* New York: Norton.

de Shazer, S. (1984). The death of resistance. *Family Process, 23*, 11–17.

de Shazer, S. (1985). *Keys to solution in brief therapy.* New York: Norton.

de Shazer, S. (1988). *Clues: Investigating solutions in brief therapy.* New York: Norton.

de Shazer, S. (1991). *Putting difference to work.* New York: Norton.

de Shazer, S. (1994). *Words were originally magic.* New York: Norton.

de Shazer, S., Berg, I. K., Lipchik, E., Nunnally, E., Molnar E., Gingerich, K., & Weiner-Davis, M. (1986). Brief therapy: Focused solution development. *Family Process, 25*, 207–222.

de Silva, P. (2004). Jealousy in couple relationships. *Behaviour Change, 21*, 1–13.

Doerries, D. B., & Foster, V. A. (2001). Family counselors as school consultants: Where are the solutions? *The Family Journal: Counseling and Therapy for Couples and Families, 9*, 391–397.

Diefenbach, G. J., Reitman, D., & Williamson, D. A. (2000). Trichotillomania: A challenge to research and practice. *Clinical Psychology Review, 20*, 289–309.

Dimond, R. E., Havens, R. A., & Jones, A. C. (1978). A conceptual framework for the practice of prescriptive eclecticism in psychotherapy. *American Psychologist, 33*, 239–248.

Dolan, M., & Bishay, N. R. (1996). The role of the sexual behaviour/attractiveness schema in morbid jealousy. *Journal of Cognitive Psychotherapy, 10*, 41–61.

Duffy, M., Gillig, S. E., Tureen, R. M., & Ybarra, M. A. (2002). A critical look at the *DSM–IV. Journal of Individual Psychology, 58*, 363–373.

Duncan, B. L., Miller, S. D., & Sparks, J. A. (2004). *The heroic client: A revolutionary way to improve effectiveness through client-directed, outcome-informed therapy.* San Francisco: Jossey-Bass.

Ellis, A. (1977). Rejoinder. Elegant and inelegant RET. *The Counseling Psychologist, 7*, 73–82.

Ellis, A. (1985). *Overcoming resistance: Rational-emotive therapy with difficult clients.* New York: Springer.

Ellis, A. (1991). The revised ABC's of rational-emotive therapy (RET). *Journal of Rational-Emotive and Cognitive Behavior Therapy, 9,* 138–172.

Ellis, A. (1996a). *Better, deeper, and more enduring brief therapy: The rational emotive behavior therapy approach.* New York: Brunner/Mazel.

Ellis, A. (1996b, August). Postmodernity or reality? A response to Allen E. Ivey, Don C. Locke, and Sandra Rigazio-DiGilio. *Counseling Today,* pp. 26–27.

Ellis, A. (1996c). A social constructionist position for mental health counseling: A reply to Jeffrey T. Guterman. *Journal of Mental Health Counseling, 18,* 16–28.

Ellis, A. (1996d). The treatment of morbid jealousy: A rational emotive behavior therapy approach. *Journal of Cognitive Psychotherapy, 10,* 23–33.

Ellis, A. (1997a). Postmodern ethics for active-directive counseling and psychotherapy. *Journal of Mental Health Counseling, 19,* 211–225.

Ellis, A. (1997b). Response to Jeffrey T. Guterman's response to my critique of his article, "A social constructionist position for mental health counseling." *Journal of Mental Health Counseling, 19,* 57–63.

Ellis, A. (2000). A continuation of the dialogue about counseling in the postmodern era. *Journal of Mental Health Counseling, 22,* 97–106.

Epstein, E. S., & Loos, V. E. (1989). Some irreverent thoughts on the limits of family therapy: Toward a language-based explanation of human systems. *Journal of Family Psychology, 2,* 405–421.

Erickson, M. H. (1967). Special techniques of brief hypnotherapy. In J. Haley (Ed.), *Advanced techniques of hypnosis and therapy: Selected papers of Milton H. Erickson, MD* (pp. 3–25). New York: Grune & Stratton.

Erickson, M. H. (1980). Further clinical techniques of hypnosis: Utilization techniques. In E. L. Rossi (Ed.), *The collected papers of Milton H. Erickson: Vol. 1* (pp. 177–205). New York: Irvington.

Fisch, R., Weakland, J. H., & Segal, L. (1982). *The tactics of change: Doing therapy briefly.* San Francisco: Jossey-Bass.

Foucault, M. (1987). *Power/knowledge: Selected interviews and writings, 1972–1977* (C. Gordon, Trans.). New York: Pantheon Books.

Fraser, J. S. (1984). Process level integration: Corrective vision for a binocular view. *Journal of Strategic and Systemic Therapies, 3,* 43–57.

Friman, P. C. (1992). Further comments on trichotillomania. *American Journal of Psychiatry, 149,* 284–285.

Gay, P. (1988). *Freud: A life for our time.* New York: Norton.

Geertz, C. (1973). *Interpretation of cultures.* New York: Basic Books.

Genette, R. (1980). *Narrative discourse.* Ithaca, NY: Cornell University Press.

Gergen, K. J. (1985). The social constructionist movement in modern psychology. *American Psychologist, 40,* 266–275.

Gergen, K. J. (1994). Exploring the postmodern: Perils or potentials. *American Psychologist, 49,* 412–416.

Gilliland, B. E., James, R. K., & Bowman, J. T. (1994). Response to the Lazarus and Beutler article "On technical eclecticism." *Journal of Counseling & Development, 72,* 554–555.

Gilroy, P., Carroll, L., & Murra, J. (2002). A preliminary survey of psychologists' personal experiences with depression and treatment. *Professional Psychology: Research and Practice, 33*, 402–407.

Gingerich, W., & Eisengart, S. (2000). Solution-focused brief therapy: A review of the outcome research. *Family Process, 39*, 477–498

Ginter, E. J. (1988). Stagnation in eclecticism: The need to recommit to a journey. *Journal of Mental Health Counseling, 10*, 3–8.

Ginter, E. J. (1989a). If you meet Moses/Jesus/Mohammed/Buddha (or associate editors of theory) on the road, kill them! *Journal of Mental Health Counseling, 11*, 335–344.

Ginter, E. J. (1989b). Slayers of monster-watermelons found in the mental health patch. *Journal of Mental Health Counseling, 11*, 77–85.

Ginter, E. J. (1997). Albert Ellis's theoretical ark: Reactions of a reader. *Journal of Mental Health Counseling, 19*, 226–232.

Ginter, E. J., Ellis, A., Guterman, J. T., Rigazio-DiGilio, S. A., Locke, D. C., & Ivey, A. E. (1996, April). *Ethical issues in the postmodern era*. Workshop at the American Counseling Association's world conference, Pittsburgh, PA.

Gladding, S. T. (2004). The potential and pitfall of William Glasser's new vision for counseling. *The Family Journal: Counseling and Therapy for Couples and Families, 12*, 342–343.

Glasser, W. (1965). *Reality therapy. A new approach to psychiatry*. New York: Harper & Row.

Glasser, W. (1998). *Choice theory: A new psychology of personal freedom*. New York: Perennial.

Glasser, W. (2003). *Warning: Psychiatry can be hazardous to your mental health*. New York: Harper & Collins.

Glasser, W. (2004a). A new vision for counseling. *The Family Journal: Counseling and Therapy for Couples and Families, 12*, 339–341.

Glasser, W. (2004b). Rejoinder. *The Family Journal: Counseling and Therapy for Couples and Families, 12*, 344.

Gorman, P. (2001). Teaching diagnosis from a postmodern perspective. *Journal of Systemic Therapies, 20*(1), 3–11.

Gray, S. W., Zide, M. R., & Wilker, H. (2000). Using the solution-focused brief therapy model with bereavement groups in rural communities: Resiliency at its best. *Hospice Journal, 15*(3), 13–30.

Guarnaccia, P. J., & Rogler, L. H. (1999). Research on culture-bound syndromes: New directions. *American Journal of Psychiatry, 156*, 1322–1327.

Guidano, V. F. (1987). *Complexity of the self: A developmental approach to psychopathology and therapy*. New York: Guilford Press.

Guterman, J. T. (1991). Developing a hybrid model of rational-emotive therapy and systemic family therapy: A response to Russell and Morrill. *Journal of Mental Health Counseling, 13*, 410–413.

Guterman, J. T. (1992a). Disputation and reframing: Contrasting cognitive-change methods. *Journal of Mental Health Counseling, 14*, 440–456.

Guterman, J. T. (1992b). *Divergent therapies: Contrasting Albert Ellis's rational-emotive therapy (RET) and the Mental Research Institute's (MRI) interactional therapy: Beyond integration and toward a basis for model building with integrity.* Doctoral dissertation, Nova University, Fort Lauderdale, FL.

Guterman, J. T. (1994). A social constructionist position for mental health counseling. *Journal of Mental Health Counseling, 16,* 226–244.

Guterman, J. T. (1996a). *Doing* mental health counseling: A social constructionist re-vision. *Journal of Mental Health Counseling, 18,* 228–252.

Guterman, J. T. (1996b). Reconstructing social constructionism: A reply to Albert Ellis. *Journal of Mental Health Counseling, 18,* 29–40.

Guterman, J. T. (1996c). Tales of mental health counseling. *Journal of Mental Health Counseling, 19,* 300–306.

Guterman, J. T. (1998). Identifying pretreatment change before the first session. *Journal of Mental Health Counseling, 20,* 370–374.

Guterman, J. T. (2005). Letter to the editor. *The Family Journal: Counseling and Therapy for Couples and Families, 13,* 1–2.

Guterman, J. T., & Kirk, M. A. (1999). Mental health counselors and the Internet. *Journal of Mental Health Counseling, 21,* 309–325.

Guterman, J. T., & Leite, M. (in press). Solution-focused counseling for clients with religious and spiritual concerns. *Counseling and Values, 51.*

Guterman, J. T., Mecias, A., & Ainbinder, D. L. (2005). Solution-focused treatment of migraine headache. *The Family Journal: Counseling and Therapy for Couples and Families, 13,* 195–198.

Guterman, J. T., Myers, J. E., Weikel, W. J., Sue, D. W., Sexton, T. L., Coe, D. M., & Rigazio-DiGilio, S. A. (1997, April). *Reflections of our image.* Workshop at the American Counseling Association's world conference, Orlando, FL.

Haley, J. (1976). *Problem-solving therapy.* New York: Harper & Row.

Hansen, J. T. (2002). Postmodern implications for theoretical integration of counseling approaches. *Journal of Counseling & Development, 80,* 315–321.

Harris, G. A. (1991). Eclecticism, again. *Journal of Mental Health Counseling, 13,* 427–431.

Hatchett, G. T. (2004). Reducing premature termination in university counseling centers. *Journal of College Student Psychotherapy, 19*(2), 13–27.

Hawkes, D., Marsh, T. I., & Wilgosh, R. (1998). *Solution-focused therapy. A handbook for healthcare professionals.* Boston: Butterworth-Heinemann.

Held, B. S. (1984). Toward a strategic eclecticism: A proposal. *Psychotherapy, 21,* 232–241.

Held, B. S. (1986). The relationship between individual psychologies and strategic/systemic therapies reconsidered. In D. E. Efron (Ed.), *Journeys: Expansion of the strategic-systemic therapies* (pp. 222–260). New York: Brunner/Mazel.

Held, B. S. (1990). What's in a name? Some confusions and concerns about constructivism. *Journal of Marital and Family Therapy, 16,* 179–186.

Held, B. S. (1991). The process/content distinction in psychotherapy revisited. *Psychotherapy, 28,* 207–217.

Held, B. S. (1992). The problem of strategy within the systemic therapies. *Journal of Marital and Family Therapy, 18,* 25–35.

Held, B. S. (1995). *Back to reality: A critique of postmodern theory in psychotherapy.* New York: Norton.

Held, B. S., & Pols, E. (1985). The confusion about epistemology and "epistemology"—and what to do about it. *Family Process, 24,* 509–517.

Hershenson, D. B. (1992). A genuine copy of a fake Dior: Mental health counseling's pursuit of pathology. *Journal of Mental Health Counseling, 14,* 419–421.

Hershenson, D. B., Power, P. W., & Seligman, L. (1989a). Counseling theory as a projective test. *Journal of Mental Health Counseling, 11,* 273–279.

Hershenson, D. B., Power, P. W., & Seligman, L. (1989b). Mental health counseling theory: Present status and future prospects. *Journal of Mental Health Counseling, 11,* 44–69.

Hoffman, L. (1990). Constructing realities: An art of lenses. *Family Process, 29,* 1–12.

Hollon, S. D., Thase, M. E., & Markowitz, J. C. (2002). Treatment and prevention of depression. *Psychological Science in the Public Interest, 3*(2), 39–77.

Howard, G. S. (1991). Culture tales: A narrative approach to thinking, cross-cultural psychology, and psychotherapy. *American Psychologist, 46,* 187–197.

Hoyt, M. F. (2002). Solution-focused couples therapy. In A. S. Gurman, & M. S. Jacobson (Eds.), *Clinical handbook of couples therapy* (3rd ed., pp. 335–369). New York: Guilford Press.

Huber, C. H., & Baruth, L. G. (1989). *Rational-emotive family therapy: A systems perspective.* New York: Springer.

Ivey, A. E. (1989). Mental health counseling: A developmental process and profession. *Journal of Mental Health Counseling, 11,* 26–35.

Ivey, A. E. (2000). *Developmental therapy.* Framingham, MA: Microtraining Associates.

Ivey, A. E., & Ivey, M. B. (2003). *Intentional interviewing and counseling: Facilitating client development in a multicultural society* (5th ed.). Pacific Grove, CA: Brooks/Cole.

Ivey, A. E., Locke, D. C., & Rigazio-DiGilio, S. A. (1996, June). The spirit and the challenge: Postmodernity or reality? *Counseling Today,* p. 33.

Johnson, L. D., & Miller, S. D. (1994). Modification of depression risk factors: A solution-focused approach. *Psychotherapy: Theory, Research, Practice, Training, 31,* 244–253.

Joyce-Moniz, L. (1985). Epistemological therapy and constructivism. In M. J. Mahoney & A. Freeman (Eds.), *Cognition and psychotherapy* (pp. 143–179). New York: Plenum Press.

Kant, I. (1929). *The critique of pure reason* (N. K. Smith, Trans.). New York: Macmillan.

Kazdin, A. E. (1996). Dropping out of child psychotherapy: Issues for research and implications for practice. *Clinical Child Psychology and Psychiatry, 1,* 133–156.

Keenan, P. S., & Farrell, D. P. (2000). Treating morbid jealousy with eye movement desensitization and reprocessing utilizing cognitive interweave: A case report. *Counseling Psychology Quarterly, 13*, 175–189.

Keeney, B. P. (1983). *Aesthetics of change.* New York: Guilford Press.

Kelly, G. (1955). *The psychology of personal constructs.* New York: Norton.

Kelly, K. R. (1988). Defending eclecticism: The utility of informed choice. *Journal of Mental Health Counseling, 10*, 210–213.

Kelly, K. R. (1991). Theoretical integration is the future for mental health counseling. *Journal of Mental Health Counseling, 13*, 106–111.

Kiser, D. J., Piercy, F. P., & Lipchik, E. (1993). The integration of emotion in solution-focused therapy. *Journal of Marital and Family Therapy, 19*, 233–242.

Klingman, A. (2002). From supportive-listening to a solution-focused intervention for counsellors dealing with political trauma. *British Journal of Guidance and Counselling, 30*, 247–259.

Kress, V. E. W., Eriksen, K. P., & Rayle, A. D., & Ford, S. J. W. (2005). The *DSM–IV–TR* and culture: Considerations for counselors. *Journal of Counseling & Development, 83*, 97–104.

Kubler-Ross, E. (1969). *On death and dying.* New York: Macmillan.

Kurzweil, R. (2005). *The singularity is near: When humans transcend biology.* New York: Viking Books.

Lakoff, G., & Johnson, M. (1980). *Metaphors we live by.* Chicago: University of Chicago Press.

Lawson, D. (1994). Identifying pretreatment change. *Journal of Counseling & Development, 72*, 244–248.

Lazarus, A. A. (1997). *Brief but comprehensive psychotherapy: The multimodal way.* New York: Springer.

Lazarus, A. A., & Beutler, L. E. (1993). On technical eclecticism. *Journal of Counseling & Development, 71*, 381–385.

Lee, C. (2001). Defining and responding to racial and ethnic diversity. In D. C. Locke, J. E. Myers, & E. L. Herr (Eds.), *The handbook of counseling* (pp. 581–588). Thousand Oaks, CA: Sage.

Liddle, H. A. (1982). On the problem of eclecticism: A call for epistemologic clarification and human-scale theories. *Family Process, 21*, 243–250.

Lipchik, E. (2002). *Beyond technique in solution-focused therapy: Working with emotions and the therapeutic relationship.* New York: Guilford Press.

Lipchik, E., & Kubicki, A. D. (1996). Solution-focused domestic violence views: Bridges toward a new reality in couples therapy. In S. D. Miller, M. A. Hubble, & B. L. Duncan (Eds.), *Handbook of solution-focused brief therapy* (pp. 65–98). San Francisco: Jossey-Bass.

Lonner, W. J., & Ibrahim, A. A. (2002). Appraisal and assessment in cross-cultural counseling. In P. B. Pedersen, J. G. Draguns, W. L. Lonner, & J. E. Trimble (Eds.), *Counseling across cultures* (5th ed., pp. 355–379). Thousand Oaks, CA: Sage.

Mahoney, M. J. (1985). Psychotherapy and human change processes. In M. J. Mahoney & A. Freeman (Eds.), *Cognition and psychotherapy* (pp. 3–48). New York: Plenum Press.

Mair, M. (1988). Psychology as storytelling. *International Journal of Personal Construct Psychology, 1*, 125–138.

Marlatt, G. A., & Donovan, D. M. (2005). *Relapse prevention: Maintenance strategies in the treatment of addictive behaviors* (2nd ed.). New York: Guilford Press.

Marlatt, G. A., & Gordon, J. (Eds.). (1985). *Relapse prevention.* New York: Guilford Press.

Marsella, A. J., & Kaplan, A. (2002). Cultural considerations for understanding, assessing, and treating depressive experience and disorder. In M. A. Reinecke & M. R. Davison (Eds.), *Comparative treatments of depression* (pp. 47–78). New York: Springer.

Mason, W. H., Chandler, M. C., & Grasso, B. C. (1995). Solution-based techniques applied to addictions: A clinic's experience in shifting paradigms. *Alcoholism Treatment Quarterly, 13*(4), 39–49.

Maturana, H. R., & Varela, F. J. (1988). *The tree of knowledge: The biological roots of human understanding.* Boston: New Science Library.

McBride, M. C., & Martin, G. E. (1990). A framework for eclecticism: The importance of theory to mental health counseling. *Journal of Mental Health Counseling, 12*, 495–505.

Meichenbaum, D. (1977). *Cognitive-behavior modification: An integrative approach.* New York: Plenum Press.

Michael, K. D. (2004). Behavioral treatment of trichotillomania: A case study. *Clinical Case Studies, 3*, 171–182.

Miller, G., & de Shazer, S. (2000). Emotions in solution-focused therapy: A reexamination. *Family Process, 39*, 5–23.

Miller, S. D. (1992). The symptoms of solution. *Journal of Strategic and Systemic Therapies, 11*(1), 1–11.

Molnar A., & de Shazer, S. (1987). Solution-focused therapy: Toward the identification of therapeutic tasks. *Journal of Marital and Family Therapy, 13*, 349–358.

Mulinari-Brenner, F., & Bergfeld, W. F. (2001). Hair loss: An overview. *Dermatology Nursing, 13*, 269–274.

Murphy, J. J. (1997). *Solution-focused counseling in middle and high schools.* Alexandria, VA: American Counseling Association.

Murray, C. J. L., & Lopez, A. D. (1997). Global mortality, disability, and the contribution of risk factors: Global Burden of Disease Study. *Lancet, 349*, 1346–1442.

Myers, J. E., & Harper, M. C. (2004). Evidence-based effective practices with older adults. *Journal of Counseling & Development, 82*, 207–218.

Nance, D. W., & Meyers, P. (1991). Continuing the eclectic journey. *Journal of Mental Health Counseling, 13*, 119–130.

Ness, M. E., & Murphy, J. J. (2002). Pretreatment change reports by clients in a university counseling center: Relationship to inquiry technique, client, and situational variables. *Journal of College Counseling, 4*(1), 20–31.

Norcross, J. C. (2000). Here comes the self-help revolution in mental health. *Psychotherapy: Theory, Research, Practice, Training, 37*, 370–377.

Nordhus, I. H., & VandenBos, G. R. (Eds.). (1998). *Clinical gero-psychology.* Washington, DC: American Psychological Association.

O'Hanlon, B. (2004). *Thriving through crisis: Turn tragedy and trauma into growth and change.* New York: Perigee Books.

O'Hanlon, W. H., & Weiner-Davis, M. (1989). *In search of solutions: A new direction in psychotherapy.* New York: Norton.

O'Hanlon, W. H., & Wilk, J. (1987). *Shifting contexts: The generation of effective psychotherapy.* New York: Guilford Press.

Palmer, C. J., Yates, W. R., & Trotter, L. (1999). Childhood trichotillomania: Successful treatment with fluoxetine following an SSRI failure. *Psychosomatics, 40,* 526–528.

Paradise, L. V., & Kirby, P. C. (2005). The treatment and prevention of depression: Implications for counseling and counselor training. *Journal of Counseling & Development, 83,* 116–119.

Paul, G. L. (1967). Strategy of outcome research in psychotherapy. *Journal of Consulting Psychology, 31,* 109–119.

Pedersen, P. (1990). The multicultural perspective as a fourth force in counseling. *Journal of Mental Health Counseling, 12,* 93–95.

Pedersen, P. (Ed.). (1998). *Multiculturalism as a fourth force.* Philadelphia: Taylor & Francis.

Petrocelli, J. V. (2002). Processes and stages of change: Counseling with the transtheoretical model of change. *Journal of Counseling & Development, 80,* 22–30.

Piaget, J. (1954). *The construction of reality in the child.* New York: Basic Books.

Pichot, T. (2001). Cocreating solutions for substance abuse. *Journal of Systemic Therapies, 20*(2), 1–23.

Piercy, F. P., Lipchik, E., & Kiser, D. (2000). Miller and de Shazer's article on "Emotions in solution-focused therapy." *Family Process, 39,* 25–28.

Pines, A. M. (1992). Romantic jealousy: Five perspectives and an integrative approach. *Psychotherapy: Theory, Research, Practice, Training, 29,* 675–683.

Pope, M. (2004). Professional counseling and Dr. Glasser: A relationship based on reality and choice. *The Family Journal: Counseling and Therapy for Couples and Families, 12,* 345–349.

Pote, H., Stratton, P., Cottrell, D., Shapiro, D., & Boston, P. (2003). Systemic family therapy can be manualized: Research process and findings. *Journal of Family Therapy, 25,* 236–262.

Prochaska, J. O., & DiClemente, C. C. (1982). Transtheoretical therapy: Toward a more integrative model of change. *Psychotherapy: Theory, Research, and Practice, 19,* 276–288.

Quick, E. K. (1996). *Doing what works in brief therapy: A strategic solution-focused approach.* San Diego, CA: Academic Press.

Ramirez, M. (1999). *Multicultural psychotherapy: An approach to individual and cultural differences* (2nd ed.). Needham Heights, MA: Allyn & Bacon.

Rigazio-DiGilio, S. A. (2001). Postmodern theories of counseling. In D. C. Locke, J. Myers, & E. L. Herr (Eds.), *The handbook of counseling* (pp. 197–218). Thousand Oaks, CA: Sage.

Rigazio-DiGilio, S. A., Ellis, A., D'Andrea, M., Guterman, J. T. , & Ivey, A. E. (1999, April). *Counseling in the postmodern era.* Workshop at the American Counseling Association's world conference, San Diego, CA.

Rigazio-DiGilio, S. A., Ivey, A. E., & Locke, D. C. (1997). Continuing the postmodern dialogue: Enhancing and contextualizing multiple voices. *Journal of Mental Health Counseling, 19,* 233–255.

Riskind, J. H. (2005). Cognitive mechanisms in generalized anxiety disorder: A second generation of theoretical perspectives. *Cognitive Therapy and Research, 29*(1), 1–5.

Robbins, A. (1997). *Unlimited power: The new science of personal achievement.* New York: Fireside.

Rogers, C. (1951). *Client-centered therapy.* Boston: Houghton Mifflin.

Rudes, J., & Guterman, J. T. (2005). Doing counseling: Bridging the modern and postmodern paradigms. In G. R. Waltz & R. Yep (Eds.), *VISTAS: Compelling perspectives in counseling 2005* (pp. 7–10). Alexandria, VA: American Counseling Association.

Russell, B. (1950). *The conquest of happiness.* New York: New American Library.

Russell, T. T., & Morrill, C. M. (1989). Adding a systemic touch to rational-emotive therapy for families. *Journal of Mental Health Counseling, 11,* 184–192.

Rygh, J. L., & Sanderson, W. C. (2004). *Treating generalized anxiety disorder: Evidence-based strategies, tools, and techniques.* New York: Guilford Press.

Santa, R. E. (1995). Utilizing solution-focused counseling for students on academic probation. *Journal of College Student Psychotherapy, 10*(2), 39–53.

Schopenhauer, A. (1907). *The will in nature.* London: Bell.

Sharry, J., Darmody, M., & Madden, B. (2002). A solution-focused approach to working with clients who are suicidal. *British Journal of Guidance & Counselling, 20,* 383–399.

Shilts, L., Rambo, A., & Huntley, E. (2003). The collaborative miracle: When to slow down the pace of brief therapy. *Journal of Systemic Therapies, 22,* 65–73.

Siewiorek, D. P., & Hamilton, C. (2003). *Wearable computers.* Wellesley, MA: Peters.

Simon, G. M. (1989). An alternative defense of eclecticism: Responding to Kelly and Ginter. *Journal of Mental Health Counseling, 11,* 280–288.

Simon, G. M. (1991). Theoretical eclecticism: A goal we are obliged to pursue. *Journal of Mental Health Counseling, 13,* 112–118.

Sklare, G. B. (2005). *Brief counseling that works: A solution-focused approach for school counselors and administrators* (2nd ed.).Thousand Oaks, CA: Corwin Press.

Smith, D. (1982). Trends in counseling and psychotherapy. *American Psychologist, 37,* 802–809.

Softas-Nall, B. C., & Francis, P. C. (1998a). A solution-focused approach to a family with a suicidal member. *The Family Journal: Counseling and Therapy for Couples and Families, 6,* 227–230.

Softas-Nall, B. C., & Francis, P. C. (1998b). A solution-focused approach to suicide assessment and intervention with families. *The Family Journal: Counseling and Therapy for Couples and Families, 6,* 64–66.

Stein, D. J., Christenson, G. A., & Hollander, E. H. (Eds.). (1999). *Tricho-tillomania*. Washington, DC: American Psychiatric Press.

Stein, D. J., Hollander, E., & Josephson, S. C. (1994). Serotonin reuptake blockers for the treatment of obsessional jealousy. *Journal of Clinical Psychiatry, 55*(1), 30–33.

Sue, D. W., & Sue, D. (1990). *Counseling the culturally different: Theory and practice* (2nd ed.). New York: Wiley.

Talmon, M. (1990). *Single-session therapy: Maximizing the effect of the first (and often only) therapeutic encounter*. San Francisco: Jossey-Bass.

Tang, T. Z., & DeRubeis, R. J. (1999). Sudden gains and critical sessions in cognitive–behavioral therapy for depression. *Journal of Consulting and Clinical Psychology, 67*, 894–904.

Tang, T. Z., Luborsky, L., & Andrusyna, T. (2002). Sudden gains in recovering from depression: Are they also found in psychotherapies other than cognitive–behavioral therapy? *Journal of Consulting and Clinical Psychology, 70*(2), 444–447.

Tarrier, N., Beckett, R., & Harwood, S. (1990). Morbid jealousy: A review and cognitive–behavioural formulation. *British Journal of Psychiatry, 157*, 319–326.

Thakker, J., Ward, T., & Strongman, K. T. (1999). Mental disorder and cross-cultural psychology: A constructivist perspective. *Clinical Psychology Review, 19*, 843–874.

Throckmorton, W., Best, J. D., & Alison, K. (2001). Does a prompting statement impact client-reported pretreatment change? An empirical investigation. *Journal of Mental Health Counseling, 23*, 48–56.

Toffler, A. (1970). *Future shock*. New York: Bantam

Toffler, A. (1980). *The third wave*. New York: Bantam.

Torres, J. B. (1998). Masculinity and gender roles among Puerto Rican men: A dilemma for Puerto Rican men's personal identity. *American Journal of Orthopsychiatry, 68*, 16–26.

Torres, J. B., Solberg, V. S. H., & Carlstrom, A. H. (2002). The myth of sameness among Latino men and their machismo. *American Journal of Orthopsychiatry, 72*, 163–181.

Tyler, L. E. (1953). *The work of the counselor*. New York: Appleton-Century-Crofts.

Vaihinger, H. (1924). *The philosophy of "as if."* London, England: Routledge & Kegan Paul.

Varela, F. J. (1979). *Principles of biological autonomy*. New York: Elsevier North Holland.

Vico, G. (1948). *The new science* (T. G. Bergin & M. H. Fisch, Trans.). Ithaca, NY: Cornell University Press.

Videbech, P., Ravnkilde, B., & Fiirgaard, B. (2001). Structural brain abnormalities in unselected in-patients with major depression. *Acta Psychiatrica Scandinavica, 103*(4), 282–286.

von Foerster, H. (1984). On constructing a reality. In P. Watzlawick (Ed.), *The invented reality: How do we know what we really know? Contributions to constructivism* (pp. 41–61). New York: Norton.

142

Walter, J., & Peller, J. (1993). Solution-focused brief therapy. *The Family Journal: Counseling and Therapy for Couples and Families, 1,* 80–81.

Watzlawick, P. (Ed.). (1984). *The invented reality: How do we know what we really know? Contributions to constructivism.* New York: Norton.

Watzlawick, P., Beavin, J. H., & Jackson, D. D. (1967). *Pragmatics of human communication: A study of interactional patterns, pathologies, and paradoxes.* New York: Norton.

Watzlawick, P., & Coyne, J. C. (1990). Depression following stroke: Brief, problem-focused family treatment. In P. Watzlawick (Ed.), *Munchausen's pigtail* (ch. 3). New York: Norton.

Watzlawick, P., Weakland, J. H., & Fisch, R. (1974). *Change: Principles of problem formation and problem resolution.* New York: Norton.

Weakland, J. H., Fisch, R., Watzlawick, P., & Bodin, A. M. (1974). Brief therapy: Focused problem resolution. *Family Process, 13,* 141–167.

Weiner-Davis, M. (1993). *Divorce busting: A step-by-step approach to making your marriage loving again.* New York: Simon & Schuster.

Weiner-Davis, M., de Shazer, S., & Gingerich, W. (1987). Using pretreatment change to construct a therapeutic solution: An exploratory study. *Journal of Marital and Family Therapy, 13,* 359–363.

Weinrach, S. G. (1991). Selecting a counseling theory while scratching your head: A rational-emotive therapist's personal journey. *Journal of Mental Health Counseling, 13,* 367–378.

White, M. (1988, Winter). The process of questioning: A therapy of literary merit? *Dulwich Center Newsletter,* pp. 8–14.

White, M. (2000). *Reflections on narrative practice.* Adelaide, South Australia: Dulwich Center.

White, M., & Epston, D. (1990). *Narrative means to therapeutic ends.* New York: Norton.

White, V. E., Kelly, B. L., & McCormick, L. J. (2004). Trichotillomania: Assessment, diagnosis, and treatment. *Journal of Counseling & Development, 82,* 185–190.

Wittgenstein, L. (1963). *Philosophical investigations* (G. E. M. Anscombe, Trans.). New York: Macmillan.

Young, S., & Holdore, G. (2003). Using solution-focused brief therapy in individual referrals for bullying. *Educational Psychology in Practice, 19,* 271–282.

INDEX

A

ACA Code of Ethics, 46
Acknowledgment in grief counseling, 96, 98
Addiction, treatment of, 83–93
  See also Substance problems, treatment of
"Adding a Systemic Touch to Rational-Emotive Therapy for Families" (Russell & Morrill), xii
African American clients, 90–91
Alcoholism, treatment of, 83–93
  See also Substance problems, treatment of
Anderson, H., 17
Anderson, Walter Truett, 10
Anxiety, 103–105
Appreciative inquiry movement, 126
Artificial intelligence, 129

B

Bateson, Gregory, 22
Bateson Project, 22
Beattie, Melody, 31, 32
Berg, I.K., 83, 85, 87, 88
Better, Deeper, and More Enduring Brief Therapy (Ellis), 6
Bipolar disorder, 48, 70
Bishay, N.R., 105
Borderline personality disorder, 99–100
Brief counseling, 6–7, 61
Brief Family Therapy Center, ix, 25, 125, 126
Brief Therapy Center, 22
Butler, W.R., 96

C

Casey, J., 125
Categorization of clients, 86

Change process, 5, 27–29, 71
Client-counselor relationship
  collaborative. *See* Collaborative approach of solution-focused counseling
  counselors as participant-observers, 15–16, 27, 39–40
  methodological boundary between client and counselor, 114
Coaching, 126–127
Coconstructing of problem, 28
  in treatment of depression, 73
Coconstructing tasks, 53–56
  client's forgetting of task, 91–92, 114
  in treatment of depression, 74–75
Codependency, 31–32, 49
Codependent No More: How to Stop Controlling Others and Start Caring for Yourself (Beattie), 31, 32
Cognitive and behavioral techniques, use of, 50, 52, 71–72, 125
Cognitive restructuring, 12
Collaborative approach of solution-focused counseling, 4, 18–20, 45
Community programs for clients with substance problems, 88
Complainant as categorization of clients, 87
Confidentiality, 91
Constructivism, 10–12
Consulting colleagues, 65–66
Content, defined, 25–26
Continuing education, 64
Cooperating, 19, 20, 58, 86
Crystal Ball Technique, 51
Cultural issues and depression, 71
Customer as categorization of clients, 86–87
Cybernetics, 22–23

D

D'Andrea, Michael, xvi
DCT. *See* Developmental Counseling and Therapy
"The Death of Resistance" (deShazar), 19
Denial, 15, 86–87
Depression, treatment of, 69–82
    case example, 77–82, 109–110
    coconstructing tasks in, 56, 74–75
    conceptualization and, 70–72
    feedback loops and, 22–23, 24
    identifying and amplifying exceptions, 73–74
    medication and, 69–70
    miracle question, use of, 74
    older client with, case example, 42
    scaling techniques in, 75–76
    solution-focused approach to, 69–73
    sudden gains in, 72–73
    treatment strategies, 73–77
deShazer, Steve, vii, xiii, ix, 13, 19, 21, 25, 26–27, 31, 51, 54, 61, 62, 65, 70, 114, 124
Developmental Counseling and Therapy (DCT), vii, viii
Deviation-amplifying positive feedback loop, 23, 60
Diagnostic and Statistical Manual of Mental Disorders, fourth edition *(DSM-IV-TR),* 13–14, 16, 70, 71, 101, 103
"*Doing* Mental Health Counseling: A Social Constructionist Re-Vision" (Guterman), xiv
Dolan, M., 105
Dropouts from counseling, 66–67
Drug addiction, treatment of, 83–93
    See also Substance problems, treatment of
DSM-IV-TR. See Diagnostic and Statistical Manual of Mental Disorders, fourth edition

E

Eclecticism, 2–3
    depression, treatment of, 71
    strategic eclecticism, xiv, 3, 5–6, 29–33, 124
    use of approach, 30–31, 49, 63–64
Educational settings, use of solution-focused approach in, 125

Educative phase, 49, 50
Ellis, Albert, vii, x–xi, xii, xiv–xvi, 6, 12, 20, 31
Emotions and solution-focused counseling, 123–125
Epistemology, 9
Erickson, Milton H., 19, 22
Exceptions
    amplifying of, 28, 52–53
    defined, viii, 36
    depression treatment, identifying and amplifying in, 73–74
    identifying of, 28, 50–51, 61
    inquiring about in pretreatment intervention, 41
    morbid jealousy treatment, identifying and amplifying in, 108
    potential exceptions, identifying of, 51
    schizophrenia treatment, amplifying of, 116–117
    substance problem treatment, identifying and amplifying in, 88–89
    tasks, identifying and amplifying based on, 57–66

F

Family member's participation
    in counseling session, 115
    in pretreatment intervention, 41
Family Solutions, 128–129
Family therapy, 2
First-order change, 24
First session's clinical process, 45–56
    amplifying exceptions, 52–53
    coconstructing a problem and goal, 46–50
    coconstructing tasks, 53–56
    identifying exceptions, 50–51
    joining with the client, 33, 45–46
Fisch, Richard, 19, 22
Formal content
    defined, 26
    depression and, 70
    in solution-focused counseling, 29, 30, 49
Formal intake, 45–46
"Formula first session task," 25
Foucault, M., 61

Freud, Sigmund, 9, 123
Future orientation in grief counseling, 96, 98

G

Geertz, Clifford, 15–16
Generalized anxiety disorder, treatment
of, 103–105
Generic approach to solution-focused
counseling, 30–31, 49
in treatment of depression, 71
in treatment of morbid jealousy,
108
Gergen, K.J., 13, 126
Gerstein, Lawrence, xii
Gestalt approach, 125
Ginter, E.J., 14, 15, 16, 17, 18, 29
Glasser, William, 32
Goolishian, H., 17
Grief, treatment of, 56, 95–98
Guterman, Jeffrey T., vii–viii, xiii

H

Hair pulling, treatment of, 100–103
Haley, Jay, 22, 47
Harper, M.C., 41
Held, B.S., xiii, 25, 26, 27, 30
Helsinki Brief Therapy Institute, 126
Hidden customer, 87, 90
"Hitler remark" of Albert Ellis, xiv–xvi
Hoffman, L., 13
Howard, G.S., 17

I

*In Search of Solutions: A New Direction
in Psychotherapy* (O'Hanlon &
Weiner-Davis), 1
Inertia principles, 5
Informal content
coconstructed problem as, 28
defined, 26
in solution-focused counseling, 29–
30, 49
Intake procedure, 35, 40, 45–46
International Society for Mental Health
Online, 127
Internet, use in counseling, 41, 127–129
Interpretation of Cultures (Geertz), 15

Irrational beliefs, 29–30
See also REBT (rational emotive
behavior therapy)
Ivey, Allen, vii–viii, xiv, xv, xvi, 12, 18

J

Jackson, Don, 22
Jealousy, 105–110
Journaling, 62–63
See also Logs

K

Keeney, B.P., 16
Knowledge in social constructivism, xvi,
13
Kubler-Ross, Elizabeth, 96

L

Language-determined systems, 16–18, 28,
29, 31
Latin American culture, 107
Lawson, D., 36, 39
Lazarus, A.A., 87
Liddle, H.A., 17
Life planning, 127
Locke, Don C., xiv, xv
Logical positivism, 9
Logs
depression, use of, 76
rating of symptoms, 62
structured log, use of, 62–63
substance problems, use of, 89
Lying by client, 91

M

Machismo, 107
Mandated treatment of substance
problem, 89–93
Mapping influences of problem, 61
in grief counseling, 97
in treatment of depression, 73
Marital counseling, 55–56
morbid jealousy and, 106–108
Maturana, H.R., 11
Medication
to treat depression, 69–70

Medication *(Continued)*
    to treat schizophrenia, 112, 118
    to treat substance problems, 88
Mental health counselors, 2, 18
Mental Research Institute. *See* MRI
    (Mental Research Institute) model
Methodological boundary between client
    and counselor, 114
Miller, G., 124
Miller, S.D., 38, 83, 85, 87, 88
Minimalist approach, 64–65
Miracle question, use of, 51, 74, 104
Molnar, A., 31, 51, 54, 62, 70
Morbid jealousy, treatment of, 105–108
Morrill, C.M., xii
MRI (Mental Research Institute) model
    compared to solution-focused theory,
        xiii, 26–27
    history of, 22
    problem-focused theory of, 21, 22–25
    switching to use of, 59–61
Multiculturalism and diversity, 7
Multimodal approach to clients with
    substance problems, 87–88
Myers, J.E., 41

N

Narrative therapy approach, 52, 53
Negative feedback loop, 23
Nonproblems
    as exceptions, 27
    problem/nonproblem concept, 26
Norcross, J.C., 127

O

O'Hanlon, W.H., 1, 52
Older persons, bias against, 41–43
On Death and Dying (Kubler-Ross), 96
Ontology, 9
Oppositional behavior, treatment of,
    60–61
Organizational consultation, use of
    solution-focused approach in, 125–126

P

Participant-observer role of counselors,
    15–16, 27, 39–40

Pedersen, P., 7
Peller, J., 47
Piercy, F.P., 124
Positive feedback loop, 23
Postmodernism, 4, 10–14, 128
Powers, K.V., 96
Presuppositional questioning, 50
Pretreatment change, 35–43
    delivering interventions before first
        session, 40–41
    identifying, 37–40
Problem-determined systems, 17
Problem formation, 21, 22–25
Problem theory, 25–27
Process, defined, 25, 27
Procrastination, dealing with, 55
Psychoanalysis, 9
Psychopathology, 32

Q

Quick, E.K., 59

R

Rational emotive behavior therapy. *See*
    REBT
Reality
    in constructivism, 11–12
    in social constructivism, xvi, 14–15
*Reality Therapy: A New Approach to
    Psychiatry* (Glasser), 32
Reality therapy and involvement with
    client, 33
REBT (rational emotive behavior
    therapy), x–xii, xiv, 1, 2
    ABC theory of, xi
    shortcomings of, 20
    social reform and, xvi
    solution-focused techniques and, xiii,
        3, 6, 30, 31, 52, 71
Reframing, 12, 19, 24–25
Relapses of substance problems, learning
    from, 89
Residential treatment for clients with
    substance problems, 88
Resistance, 18–20, 58, 86–87, 114
Restorying, 52
Reteaming, 126

Rigazio-DiGilio, Sandra A., xiv, xv, xvi
Russell, Bertrand, 12
Russell, T.T., xii

S

Scaling techniques, 62
    in treatment of anxiety, 105
    in treatment of depression, 75–76
Schizophrenia, treatment of, 22, 111–122
School settings, use of solution-focused
    approach in, 125
Second-order change, 24
Second session. *See* Subsequent sessions
    (second session and others)
Self-confidence, building of, 55
Self-efficacy, 52
Self-help movement, 64, 77, 96, 126–127
Sessions, process used in. *See* First session's
    clinical process; Subsequent sessions
    (second session and others)
Sharry, J., 99
Shenjing shuairuo, 71
Singularity, 129
Small changes, 4–5, 38, 51, 58, 85–86
"A Social Constructionist Position for
    Mental Health Counseling"
    (Guterman), xiii, xiv
Social constructivism, 12–14
    basis of, xiii, 10
    client-counselor relationship in,
        15–16
    collaborative approach of, 18–20
    debate over, vii, xiv
    knowledge and, xvi, 13
    language-determined systems and,
        16–18
    reality and, xvi, 14–15
    solution-focused counseling and,
        xiv, 26
Social reform and REBT, xvi
Solution-focused counseling
    brief counseling and, 6–7
    change process in, 5, 27–29
    collaborative approach of, 4
    depression, treatment of, 69–73
    emotions' role in, 123–125
    evolution of, 1–2
    first session's clinical process, 45–56

future of, 123–130
generalized anxiety disorder,
    treatment of, 103–105
grief, treatment of, 95–98
morbid jealousy, treatment of, 105–110
MRI compared to, 26–27
new settings for, 125–127
pretreatment change and, 35–43
principles of, 3–7
relationship to REBT. *See* REBT
    (rational emotive behavior therapy)
responsiveness to multiculturalism
    and diversity, 7
schizophrenia, treatment of, 111–122
small changes leading to big results,
    4–5
solution focus of, 3–4
strategic eclecticism. *See* Strategic
    eclecticism
substance problems, treatment of,
    83–85
suicidal clients, treatment of, 98–100
technological society and, 127–129
trichotillomania, treatment of, 100–103
Solution-focused theory, 25–31
    theory of problems, 25–27
"Story repair," 17
Storytelling and depression, 71
Strategic eclecticism, xiv, 3, 5–6, 29–31,
    65, 124
    case examples of, 31–33
Structured log, use of, 62–63
Subsequent sessions (second session and
    others), 57–67
    asking about scheduling another
        session, 56, 67
    asking "what's better?", 61–62
    consulting colleagues about "stuck"
        case, 65–66
    doing less of the same, 59–61
    doing more of the same, 59
    doing something different, 65–66
    eclectic approach in, 63–64
    identifying and amplifying exceptions
        derived from tasks, 57–66
    mapping influences of problem, 61
    minimalist approach, 64–65
    scaling techniques in, 62
    structured log, use of, 62–63

Subsequent sessions *(Continued)*
    summarizing session's discussion, 64
    surprise task, use of, 63
    taking time to consider client's
        situation, 64
    terminating counseling, 66–67
Substance problems, treatment of, 83–93
    case example of mandated client, 89–93
    medication to treat, 88
    multimodal approach, 87–88
    relapses, 89
    replacing behavior, 88–89
    resistance and denial, 86–87
    small changes and, 85–86
    solution-focused conceptualization
        of, 83–85
    treatment strategies, 87–89
Sudden gains, 72–73, 109
Sue, D., 107
Sue, D.W., 107
Suicidal clients, treatment of, 98–100
Summarizing session's discussion, 64
Surprise task, use of, 63

T

Tasks. *See* Coconstructing tasks
Technological change, 127–129
Telephone contact with client prior to first
    session. *See* Pretreatment change
Terminating counseling, 6, 66–67

Theory of change, 27–29, 71
Theory of problems, 25–27
Thumb sucking, 102–103
Toffler, Alvin, 127, 129
Trichotillomania, treatment of, 100–103
Tyler, Leona, viii

U

Unique outcomes, 27

V

Visitor as categorization of clients, 87

W

Walter, J., 47
Watzlawick, Paul, 14, 19, 22, 23, 24
Weakland, John, 22, 23
Web. *See* Internet, use in counseling
Weiner-Davis, M., 1, 36, 39, 52
White, Michael, 27, 52, 53, 61
Wittgenstein, L., 124
*Working With the Problem Drinker: A
    Solution-Focused Approach* (Berg &
    Miller), 83

Y

Yakima Nation Proverb, xv